BIOMES ATLASES

DESERTS
and SEMIDESERTS

Michael Allaby, Robert Anderson, and Ian Crofton

www.heinemannraintree.com
Visit our website to find out more information about Heinemann-Raintree books.

To order:
☎ Phone 888-454-2279
🖥 Visit www.heinemannraintree.com to browse our catalog and order online.

Published in 2011 by Heinemann-Raintree books, an imprint of Capstone Global Library, LLC, Chicago, Illinois

© 2011 The Brown Reference Group Ltd.

For The Brown Reference Group Ltd:
Editorial Director: Lindsey Lowe
Managing Editor: Tim Harris
Editor: Jolyon Goddard
Original consultant: Dr. Mark Hostetler,
Department of Wildlife Ecology and Conservation, University of Florida
Designers: Reg Cox, Joan Curtis
Picture researcher: Clare Newman
Production Director: Alastair Gourlay

Printed in the USA

ISBN: 978-1-432-94175-8; 978-1-432-94184-0 (set)
14 13 12 11 10
10 9 8 7 6 5 4 3 2 1

Library of Congress Cataloging-in-Publication Data

Allaby, Michael.
  Deserts and semideserts / Michael Allaby, Robert Anderson, and Ian Crofton.
     p. cm. — (Biomes atlases)
  Includes bibliographical references and index.
  ISBN 978-1-4329-4175-8
  1. Desert ecology—Juvenile literature. 2. Desert ecology—Maps for children. I. Anderson, Robert, 1966- II. Crofton, Ian (Ian D.). III. Title.
  QH541.5.D4A44 2011
  577.54—dc22   2010012426

About this Book

The introductory pages of this book describe the biomes of the world and then the desert biome. The five main chapters look at different aspects of deserts: climate, plants, animals, people, and the future. Between the chapters are detailed maps that focus on famous or important deserts. The map pages are shown in the contents in italics, *like this*. Exclamation-point icons on the map pages draw attention to regions where the biome or its wildlife is under threat. Throughout the book you'll also find boxed stories or fact files about deserts. The icons here show what the boxes are about. Words in **bold** throughout the book are explained in the glossary at the end of the book. After the glossary is a list of books and websites for further research and an index, allowing you to find subjects anywhere in the book.

 Climate

 People

 Plants

 Future

 Animals

 Facts

 Under Threat

Contents

BIOMES OF THE WORLD

Biologists divide the living world into major zones named biomes. Each biome has its own distinctive climate, plants, and animals.

If you were to walk all the way from the north of Canada to the Amazon **rain forest**, you'd notice the wilderness changing dramatically along the way (see route marked on map to right).

Northern Canada is a freezing and barren place without trees, where only tiny brownish-green plants can survive in the icy ground. But trudge south for long enough and you enter a magical world of conifer forests, where moose, caribou, and wolves live. After several weeks, the conifers disappear, and you reach the grass-covered **prairies** of the central United States. The farther south you go, the drier the land gets and the hotter the Sun feels, until you find yourself hiking through a cactus-filled **desert**. But once you reach southern Mexico, the cacti start to disappear, and strange **tropical** trees begin to take their place. Here, the muggy air is filled with the calls of exotic birds and the drone of tropical insects. Finally, in Colombia you cross the Andes mountain range—whose chilly peaks remind you a little of your starting point—and descend into the dense, swampy jungles of the Amazon rain forest.

Desert is the driest biome. There are hot deserts and cold ones.

Taiga is made up of conifer trees that can survive freezing winters.

Scientists have a special name for the different regions—such as desert, tropical rain forest, and prairie—that you'd pass through on such a journey. They call them **biomes**. Everywhere on Earth can be classified as being in one biome or another, and the same biome often appears in lots of

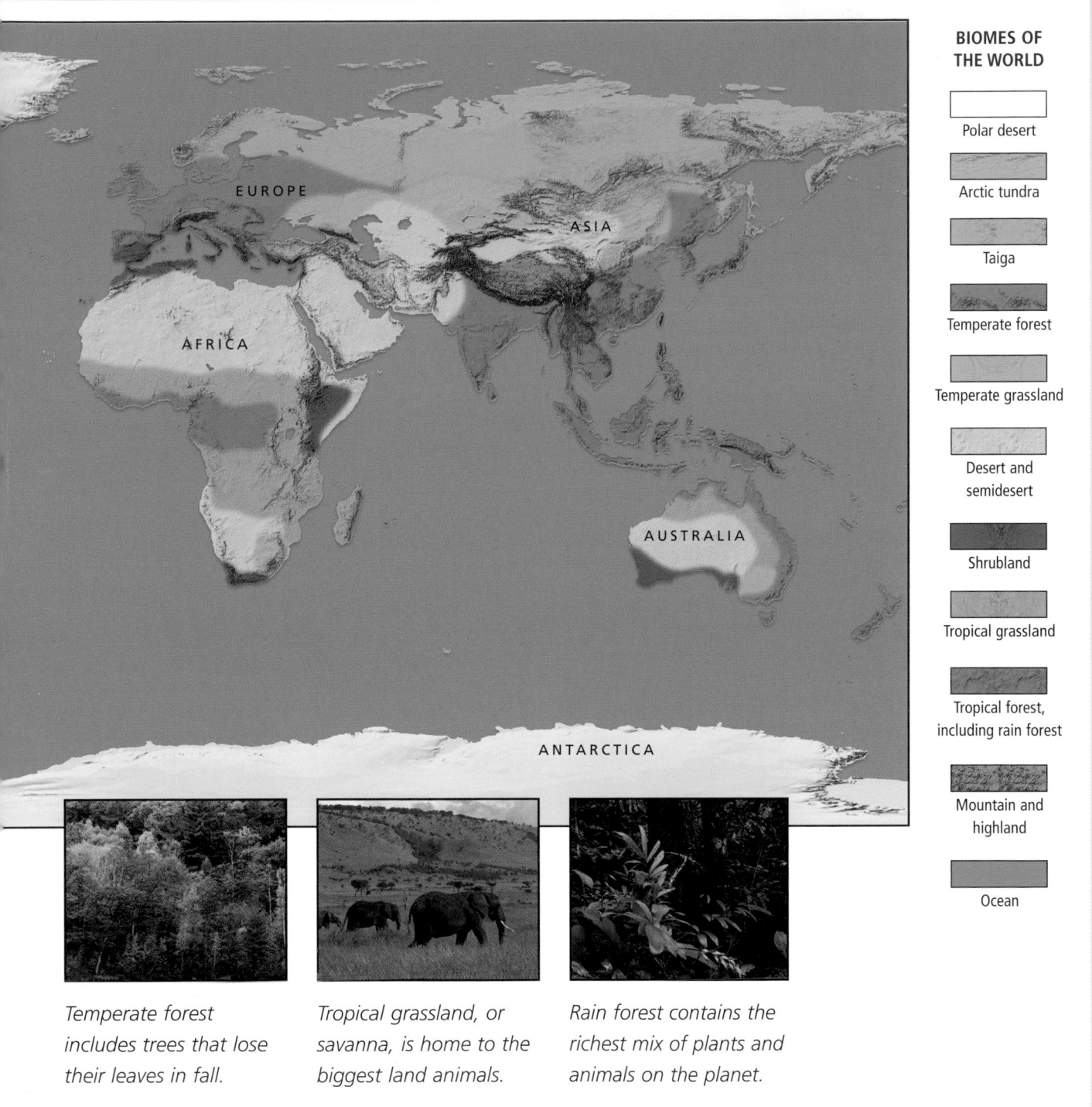

**BIOMES OF
THE WORLD**

Polar desert

Arctic tundra

Taiga

Temperate forest

Temperate grassland

Desert and
semidesert

Shrubland

Tropical grassland

Tropical forest,
including rain forest

Mountain and
highland

Ocean

*Temperate forest
includes trees that lose
their leaves in fall.*

*Tropical grassland, or
savanna, is home to the
biggest land animals.*

*Rain forest contains the
richest mix of plants and
animals on the planet.*

different places. For instance, there are areas of rain forest as far apart as Brazil, Africa, and Southeast Asia. Although the plants and animals that inhabit these forests are different, they live in similar ways. Likewise, the prairies of North America are part of the grassland biome, which also occurs in China, Australia, and Argentina. Wherever there are grasslands, there are grazing animals that feed on the grass, as well as large carnivores that hunt and kill the grazers.

The map on this page shows how the world's major biomes fit together to make up the biosphere—the zone of life on Earth.

DESERTS OF THE WORLD

There are deserts on every continent, from the sunbaked heart of Africa to the chilly plains of northern China. Together, deserts make up one of Earth's largest biomes.

Deserts come in all shapes and sizes. Some are tiny, such as the desert of Almería in southeast Spain, but others are huge. The vast arid (dry) area that spreads across North Africa, the Arabian peninsula, and western Asia is really one gigantic desert, though we give different names to different parts of it, as you can see on the map.

The world's major deserts lie in two bands near the tropics of **Cancer** and **Capricorn** (two imaginary circles around the planet, north and south of the **equator**). There are also deserts near the poles—Greenland and Antarctica are part of a biome called polar desert. You can find out more about them in the *Arctic Tundra and Polar Deserts* book.

Like most biomes, deserts do not generally have definite boundaries, except where they meet the sea or a major mountain range. In many places they merge gradually into another land biome, such as **shrubland**.

Parts of the Sonoran Desert are threatened by urban spread.

The Atacama Desert in Chile is the driest place in the world.

The land near the edge of the desert, which is not quite desert and not quite shrubland, is known as **semidesert**.

The word desert conjures up images of rolling sand dunes or plains covered in rubble, but not all deserts are like that. Parts of North America's Great Basin, for

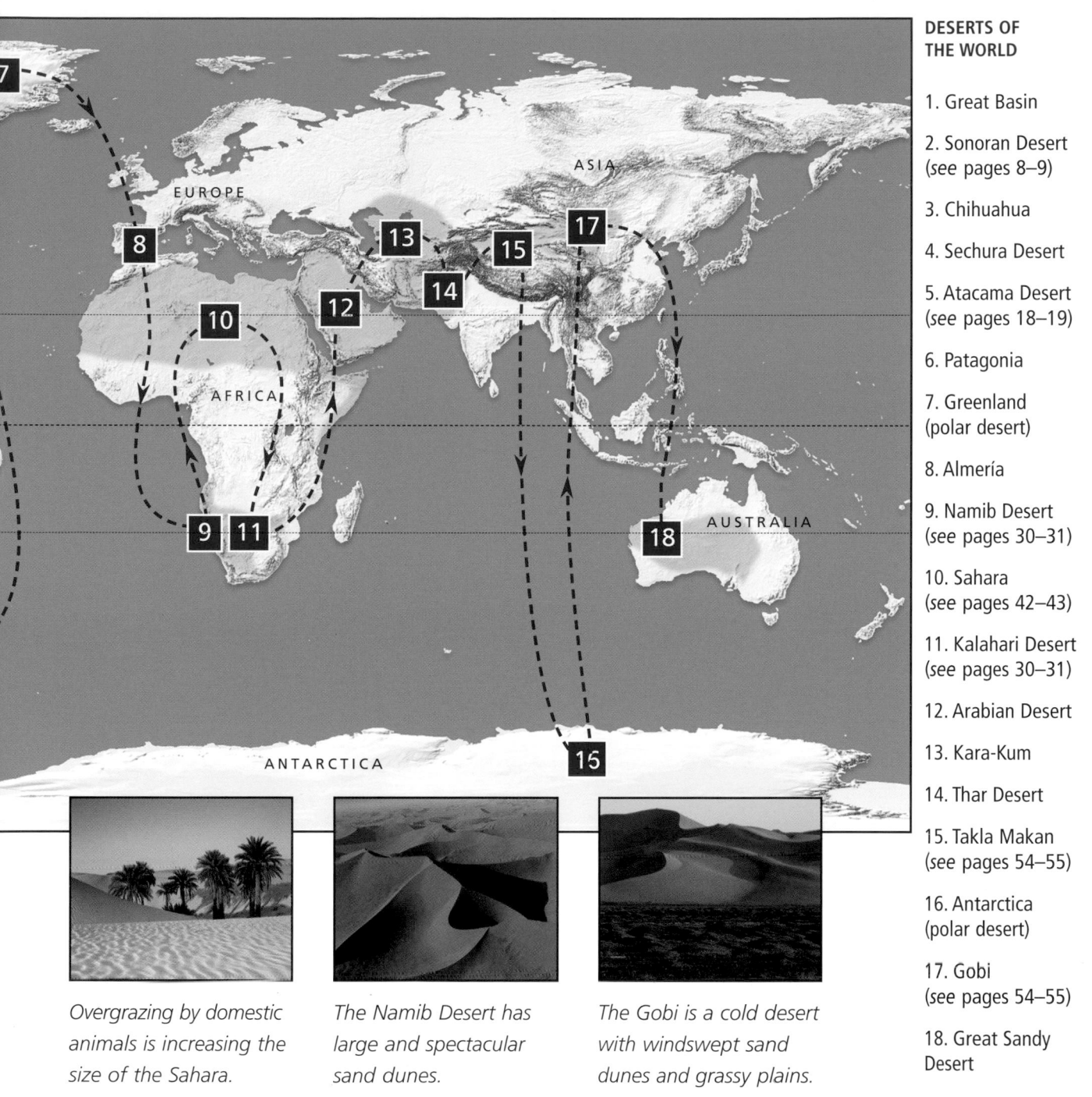

Overgrazing by domestic animals is increasing the size of the Sahara.

The Namib Desert has large and spectacular sand dunes.

The Gobi is a cold desert with windswept sand dunes and grassy plains.

instance, are completely flat and glittering white, thanks to a coating of salt crystals. The Sonoran Desert in Arizona is sometimes carpeted with colorful flowers, though only for a short time. Yet, despite their many differences, all deserts do have one thing in common: water is in very short supply.

Most biomes exist because of a distinctive pattern of weather through the year. We call these weather patterns **climates**. Tropical rain forests have a warm and wet climate, for example, while deserts have a very dry climate. So, to understand the desert biome, we need to look first at the desert climate.

SONORAN DESERT

The Sonoran Desert sprawls across the southwest United States into northern Mexico. It is the hottest North American desert but also the greenest, with forests of giant cacti.

Sonoran Facts

▲ Towering saguaro cacti and organ-pipe cacti are the most distinctive plants of this desert.

▲ Urban sprawl, new highways, and pollution are threatening regions of the Sonoran Desert.

▲ The Apache chieftain Geronimo (1829–1909) used the Sonoran Desert as a hideaway during a conflict with U.S. forces in the 19th century.

1. Mojave Desert
North of the Sonoran Desert is the Mojave Desert, home of the famously gnarled Joshua trees. Off-road vehicles are damaging parts of the Mojave Desert.

2. Colorado River
This river flows from the Rocky Mountains to Mexico, via the Grand Canyon and Sonoran Desert. The cities of Los Angeles and Phoenix get their water from the river via an aqueduct. The flow of the river has reduced because of global warming.

3. Salton Sea
A saltwater lake, formed from water running off irrigated farmland in the Imperial Valley. Various fish species have disappeared from the lake because of its increasing salinity.

4. Imperial Valley
Thousands of kilometers of irrigation canals have turned this arid valley into farmed land.

5. Yuma Desert
Sand dunes and low sandy plains dotted with creosote bushes make up this very dry part of the desert.

6. Phoenix
This city in Arizona is one of the fastest growing in the United States. However, its sprawl threatens desert wildlife.

7. Saguaro National Park
Forests of saguaro cacti cover this beautiful preserve.

8. Kitt Peak Observatory
This mountaintop observatory enjoys cloudless skies year round.

9. Organ Pipe Cactus National Monument
Organ-pipe cacti, named for their dramatic column shape, dominate this park.

10. Gulf of California
Blue and gray whales breed in the gulf. Overdevelopment of coastal regions and pollution entering the sea are threatening marine wildlife in the gulf.

11. Baja California
This region is often considered part of the Sonoran Desert.

Desert Monsters

The Sonoran Desert has more than its fair share of dangerous animals, including rattlesnakes, scorpions, and Gila monsters (left). Gila monsters are the largest lizards in North America, and the only venomous ones. They come out at night to hunt for eggs and small animals, such as mice or baby birds. When they catch a victim, they bite it and hold on. Powerful venom flows through grooves in the gila monster's teeth and into the victim's wound, paralyzing it. Fortunately, these lizards seldom bite people.

DESERT CLIMATES

Deserts exist for a very simple reason: lack of rain. But desert climates are surprisingly varied. There are hot deserts, cold deserts, polar deserts, windswept deserts, and even deserts covered with fog.

Al Azizia in Libya is probably the hottest place on Earth. On September 13, 1922, the temperature there reached 57.8°C (136°F)—the highest temperature ever recorded. That's really sizzling. The ground at Al Azizia on that day would have been hot enough to fry an egg.

Under the Burning Sun

Al Azizia is in North Africa's Sahara, one of the world's hot deserts. Not all deserts are hot, but the Sahara certainly is. Hot deserts extend all around the world in two belts, to the north and south of the tropical zone around the equator. Farther north and south are the cold deserts, and farther still in the Arctic and

Even from space, the expanses of sand in the Namib Desert are easily visible. This view is from a satellite looking south.

Antarctica are the ice-covered **polar deserts**.

All deserts are dry, since it is lack of water that makes a desert. They are dry because what little water reaches the desert **evaporates** from the ground and escapes into the **atmosphere**. Intense sunshine and hot, windy weather speed up the evaporation of water from deserts, making them even drier. But how dry is dry? Dictionaries define a desert as

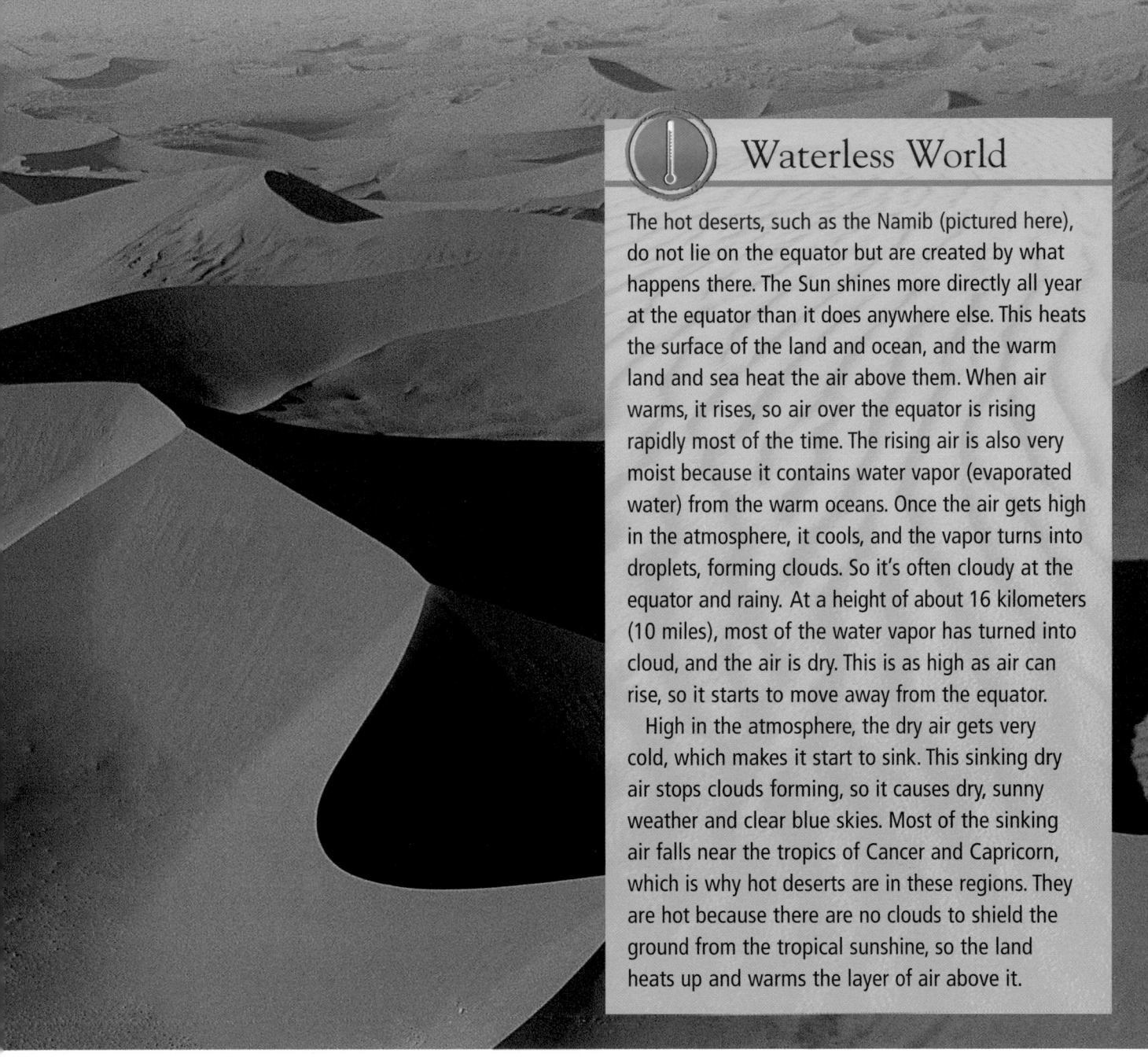

Waterless World

The hot deserts, such as the Namib (pictured here), do not lie on the equator but are created by what happens there. The Sun shines more directly all year at the equator than it does anywhere else. This heats the surface of the land and ocean, and the warm land and sea heat the air above them. When air warms, it rises, so air over the equator is rising rapidly most of the time. The rising air is also very moist because it contains water vapor (evaporated water) from the warm oceans. Once the air gets high in the atmosphere, it cools, and the vapor turns into droplets, forming clouds. So it's often cloudy at the equator and rainy. At a height of about 16 kilometers (10 miles), most of the water vapor has turned into cloud, and the air is dry. This is as high as air can rise, so it starts to move away from the equator.

High in the atmosphere, the dry air gets very cold, which makes it start to sink. This sinking dry air stops clouds forming, so it causes dry, sunny weather and clear blue skies. Most of the sinking air falls near the tropics of Cancer and Capricorn, which is why hot deserts are in these regions. They are hot because there are no clouds to shield the ground from the tropical sunshine, so the land heats up and warms the layer of air above it.

a place that receives less than 250 millimeters (10 inches) of rain a year; for comparison, the city of St. Louis, Missouri, receives about 890 millimeters (35 inches).

Some deserts receive almost no rain at all. In the town of Aswan in southern Egypt, for instance, there are many years when the rainfall is zero. On the rare occasions that it does rain in the desert, the downpour can be torrential. Intense thunderstorms quickly wet the soil surface, then further water just runs off the wet surface in sheets, creating flash floods. In the summer of 1997, heavy rain in the Atlas Mountains of Morocco caused floods that killed more than 250 people. In the same year, floods after rainstorms in northeastern Iran drowned 11 people.

Although deserts can get very hot during the day, the nights can be bitterly cold. In January, the temperature in the Sahara is high in the early afternoon, but at night it often drops below freezing. That's because dry sand and bare rock heat up quickly when the Sun shines on them, but they cool down again just as fast. And because there are no clouds to trap warmth rising from the ground, the heat soon escapes into space once the Sun has gone down.

Dust Storms and Dust Devils

Besides being dry, deserts are windy. The ferocious wind blows sand into rolling seas of dunes—it can even wear away solid rock by blasting it with sand. Sometimes the wind blows strongly enough to lift dust and sand into a vast cloud thousands of feet tall. Then it's a dust storm or sandstorm that arrives as a screaming gale, driving dust and fine sand into every corner. People caught in the open can't see and can barely breathe, because the hot air is full of choking grit.

At other times the wind plays tricks. Around the middle of the afternoon, when the ground has been heating for several hours, some places are much hotter than others. Air rising over the hot spots draws in surrounding air and starts to spiral as it rises. If the swirling, dusty air rises only a few feet, it's called a dust devil. But sometimes the swirling air rises much higher— and then it's a whirlwind.

Whirlwinds can be 1.6 kilometers (1 mile) tall. They leap up suddenly and produce howling gusts that are strong enough to smash a wooden hut. During its brief life, a whirlwind wanders about randomly—you can't tell where it will go next. It survives for only a few minutes, but as one dies down, another can leap up nearby. Long ago, before anyone knew what caused whirlwinds, desert peoples were terrified of them. Some people believed God sent whirlwinds as a punishment for sins.

Cold Deserts

When we think of deserts, it's the hot, sandy ones that spring to mind. Not all deserts are like this, though. Most of the Sahara and the deserts of Southwest Asia, for example, are covered by bare rock and gravel; the wind blows away the dust and sand. Neither are all deserts hot. The city of Hohhot in China lies on the edge of the Gobi desert. In January the temperature here averages a bitterly cold –13°C (8.6°F), and in July—the warmest month—it barely rises above room temperature. Straddling the border between Mongolia and China, the Gobi looks fairly small on a map showing the whole of Europe and Asia. In fact, it is about 1,600 kilometers (1,000 miles) from west to east. To its west is another great desert, the Takla Makan, which is about 970 kilometers (600 miles) across.

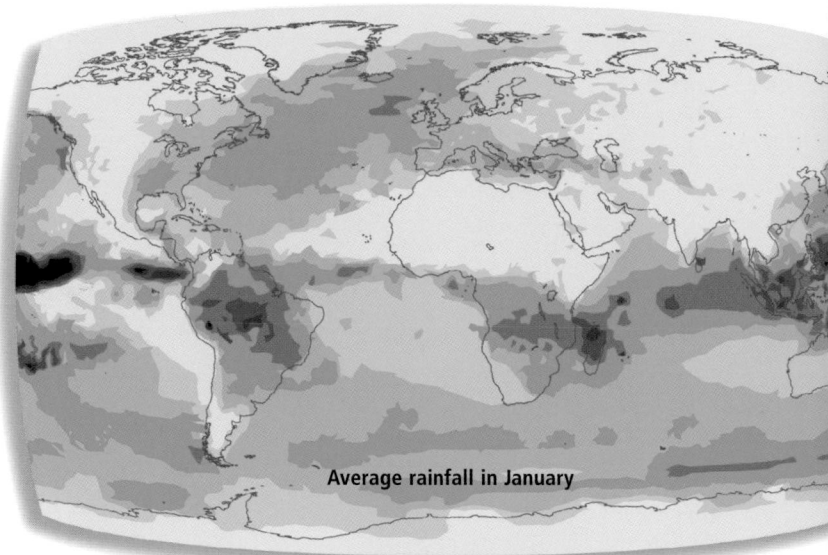

Average rainfall in January

Dark blue in these maps show areas of rain. Deserts are pale in both January and July, showing that they are dry all year round.

Average rainfall in July

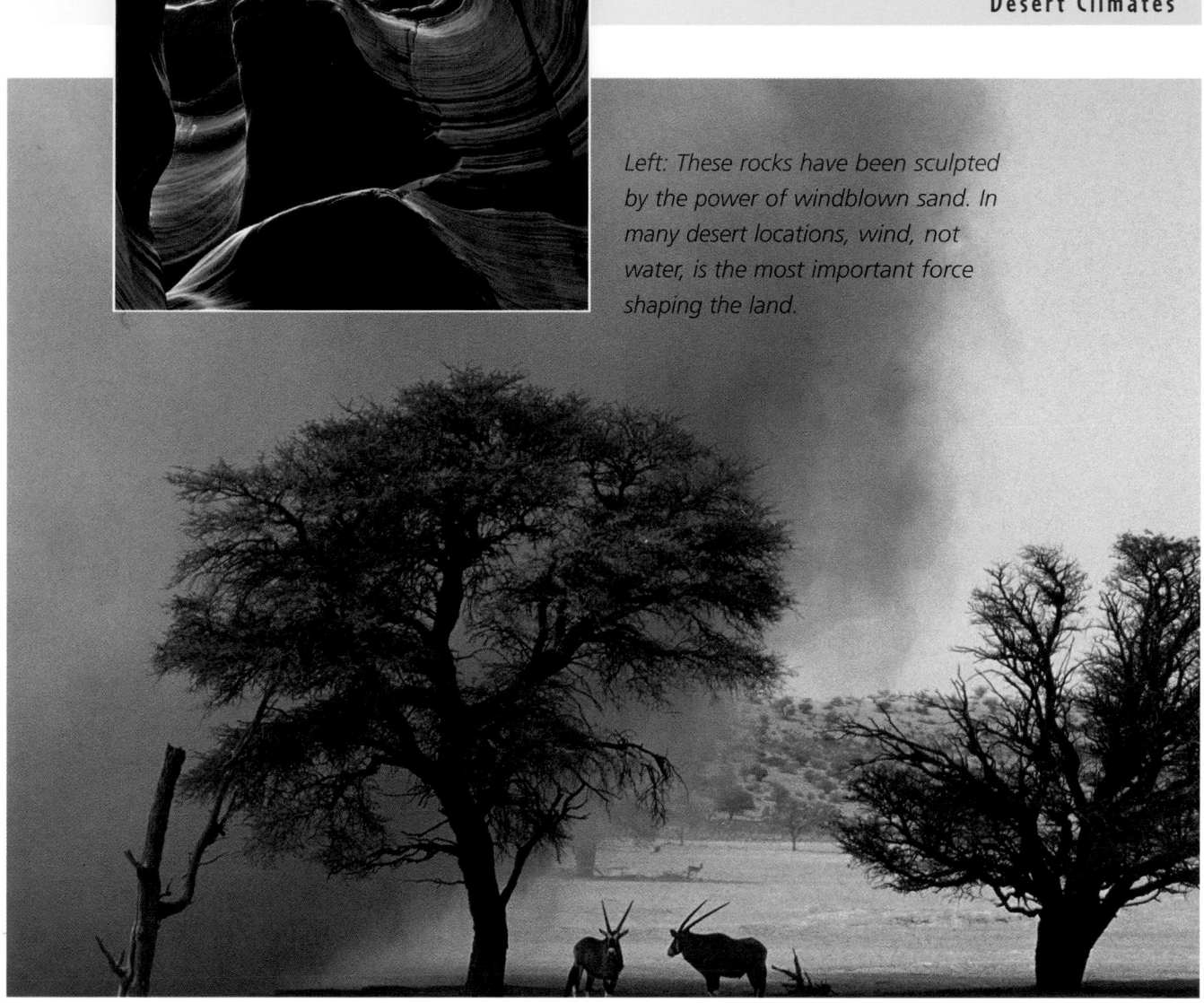

Left: These rocks have been sculpted by the power of windblown sand. In many desert locations, wind, not water, is the most important force shaping the land.

The Gobi is a harsh place—dry, windswept, and bitterly cold in winter—but the Takla Makan is much worse. In winter the temperature falls to about –24°C (–11°F), and the wind makes it feel even colder. In summer, though, the Takla Makan is hot, with temperatures around 30°C (86°F). It is a sandy desert, with great expanses of dunes that are constantly shifting between small, bare hills, where the rock has been swept clean of sand. Sandstorms are common and often last for days.

The Gobi and the Takla Makan are continental deserts: they're dry because they are thousands of kilometers from the ocean. Moist air from the sea sheds most of its water as rain on its journey inland, and then it has

Dust storms can be unpleasant and dangerous. Some animals, such as camels, close their nostrils and shield their eyes from the sand with long eyelashes. These oryx are taking cover beneath a tree.

to cross high mountains, where it loses the rest. By the time it reaches the Gobi and the Takla Makan the air is bone dry. The deserts are cold partly because they are high above sea level, but also because they are well to the north of the tropics.

By the Sea

Continental deserts are dry because they are so far inland. So you might think that a desert could never exist right next to the coast. But you'd be wrong. There are deserts like that, and they include the driest deserts of all. The Namib Desert, for instance, which runs along the coast of southwest Africa, receives about 50 millimeters (2 inches) of rain on average each year; New York receives nearly double that in a month. And certain parts of the Namib are even drier. The Namib town of Swakopmund, for instance, has an annual rainfall of only 14 millimeters (0.6 inches). The Namib is not baking, though—the daily temperature does not vary much, and is about 22°C (72°F) throughout the year.

The world's driest desert is the Atacama in South America, which stretches for about 965 kilometers (600 miles) along the coast of Chile and southern Peru. There are places in the Atacama where it has rained no more than four times a century. Iquique, a town in north Chile, once went for four years with no rain, then a single shower fell in July of the fifth year. For people in Iquique, July is now the rainy season! At Arica, to the north of Iquique, the average annual rainfall is a minuscule 0.9 millimeters (0.03 inches).

Climographs

Each place in the world has its own pattern of weather. The typical pattern of weather that happens in one place during a year is called climate. We can sum up a place's climate on a climograph, such as the one shown here for St. Louis. The letters along the bottom are the months of the year. The numbers on the left and the small bars show rainfall, and the numbers on the right and the curvy line show temperature. You can see at a glance that St. Louis is hottest in July, but December is the driest month.

14

Young Deserts

Compared to Earth's grand old age of 4.5 billion years, some of our planet's deserts are surprisingly young. The Great Basin in the United States, for instance, has been a desert for only about 12,000 years. About 15,000 years ago, forests covered the Great Basin, and mammoths, saber-toothed cats, and giant sloths roamed among the trees. When the ice age ended and the climate warmed, the desert began to form. The vast salt flats of the Great Basin, such as this one in Death Valley, are the parched remains of lakes that dried out.

Death Valley

California's Death Valley, near the edge of the Mojave Desert, is the hottest place in the United States and almost as hot as Al Azizia in Libya. The temperature in Death Valley can reach 57°C (135°F) in summer. In 1849, during the great California Gold Rush, a party of 30 settlers decided to take a shortcut to the gold fields. Their route took them through the valley, where 12 of them died from heat and thirst. That's how the valley got its name. Today Death Valley is a national park, where tourists flock to admire the scenery.

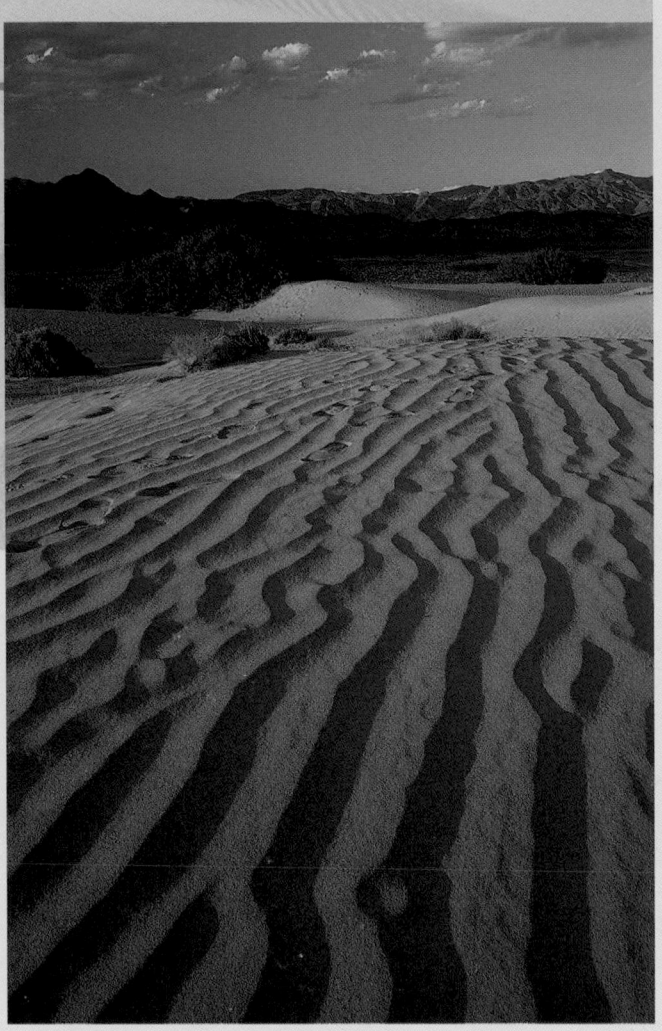

It's hard to imagine just how dry that is, but if you plan to visit you certainly won't need to pack an umbrella.

Fog but No Rain

There's something very odd about the Namib and Atacama deserts. Despite the incredibly dry climate, the air in these deserts is very moist. Fog is common, and iron objects rust quickly. So how can these deserts exist when there is so much moisture in the air?

The cause of the peculiar climates is cold ocean currents near the coasts. The cold Benguela Current flows north along the coast of the Namib Desert, and the cold Peru (or Humboldt) Current flows north along the coast of the Atacama. The chilly water cools air traveling toward the land. Because the air

Flat-topped mountains like this are called mesas.

gets cold, it stays low and doesn't rise high enough to form clouds. That's why rain is so rare. It's also why these coastal deserts are relatively cool. At Lima, Peru, the average temperature is only 19°C (66°F) and doesn't change much through the year.

Air that has crossed the ocean is very moist because it picks up a lot of water vapor. When the moist air crosses a cold ocean current and cools down, its moisture condenses into tiny droplets, forming fog. It's a bit like exhaling on a cold day—the moisture in your breath condenses into mist as it hits the cold air. The cold ocean currents near the Atacama and Namib both produce sea fogs that roll into the desert regularly. Some plants and animals get nearly all their water from the fog droplets.

Cold ocean currents tend to occur on the west coast of continents, so the Atacama and Namib are sometimes called west-coast deserts. Parts of the Sonoran Desert in Baja California and the part of the Sahara on the northwest coast of Africa are also west-coast deserts, with similar cold currents nearby.

Below: In this part of Patagonia, an ancient lava flow has been broken down by river action in an earlier, wetter time. Later, when Patagonia became a desert, the hills were eroded by wind.

Climate Change

Patagonia is a cold desert region that covers most of Argentina. It is a different kind of desert from most others. It is neither in the subtropics, nor in the centre of a big continent thousands of miles from the sea, nor on a west coast. There are two large icefields in the region—the North Patagonian and South Patagonian (below)—and these are experiencing the fastest glacial retreat anywhere on Earth. The rapid ice melt has been caused by global warming. Between 2000 and 2006 the two icefields lost 42 cubic kilometers (10 cubic miles) of ice each year—that is equivalent to the volume of 10,000 large football stadiums.

ATACAMA

The Atacama runs in a narrow strip between the Andes and the Pacific Ocean. This desert is so dry that nothing can live at its center. Life is sustained by fog in the west and by water from the Andes in the east.

 ## Atacama Facts

▲ The driest town in the world is Quillagua in the Atacama. In an average year it gets less than 0.5 millimeters (0.02 inches) of rain.

▲ Many people in the Atacama see no rain at all for years at a time. Some people have never seen rain.

▲ Millions of pelicans, petrels, penguins, and other seabirds, as well as sea lions and otters, use the desert coast to rest and breed. The emptiness of the desert protects them from land-based predators.

1. The Andes
To the east of the Atacama, the land rises toward the foothills of the Andes mountains. High peaks, including many active volcanoes, border the desert. The glaciers in the Andes are melting because of global warming.

2. Guano
The ocean off the Atacama provides the richest fishing grounds on Earth. It supports countless seabirds, which nest on land. The seabird droppings build up into deposits. People mine these deposits, called guano, to use as fertilizer. The seabird populations are decreasing, however, because of competition for fish with fishers.

3. Salar de Uyuni (Uyuni Salt Flat)
Up on the high, dry plateau of the Altiplano in Bolivia, this huge salt flat lies beyond the Atacama. Lithium mining threatens to spoil this popular tourist attraction.

4. Cordillera de la Costa
This mountain range runs along the coast. In places, the mountains end in cliffs that plunge into the ocean and provide nest sites for millions of seabirds. The forests in the mountains are threatened by deforestation and fires.

5. Chuquicamata Copper Mine
The largest open-cast copper mine on Earth and a major source of pollution in the region.

6. Valle de la Luna (Moon Valley)
The barren, gravel-strewn plains of this valley look like the surface of the Moon.

7. Peru (Humboldt) Current
This cold ocean current helps create the extreme desert conditions of the Atacama. It also creates fog.

8. Mount Ojos del Salado
At 6,880 meters (22,573 feet), this is the highest active volcano in the world.

 ## Morbid Mummies

Amazingly, people have lived in the Atacama for at least 10,000 years. At first they lived on fish, shellfish, and sea-lion meat, but later they irrigated land to grow corn and potatoes. As long ago as 5000 B.C.E., the Chinchorro people began mummifying their dead. They first took the corpse apart and removed the flesh from the bones. Then they reassembled the skeleton and replaced the internal organs with bundles of reeds. They replaced the skin, and added patches of sealskin to cover any gaps. The mummy was finished with a decorative clay mask and a wig made from hair.

N

Juliaca

PERU

Arequipa

Tacna

Arica

Pacific

Ocean

The strange moonlike landscape of Valle de la Luna makes this valley a popular tourist site in the Atacama.

7

Potosí

Salar de Uyuni

BOLIVIA

1

Iquique

2

4

Quillagua

Mount Aucanquilcha

Ollagüe Volcano

San Pedro Volcano

3

Tocopilla

Chuquicamata

5

Calama

Antofagasta

Salar de Atacama

Valle de la Luna

6

Mount Zapaleri

Mount Rincón

San Salvador de Jujuy

Salta

7

Llullaillaco

Salar de Arizaro

Azufre Volcano

CHILE

ARGENTINA

Copiapó

1

8

Mount Ojos del Salado

Atacama Desert

Cordillera de la Costa

Cordillera Domeyka

Andes

Peru Current

SOUTH AMERICA

1

200 miles

0

0   200   kilometers

DESERT PLANTS

How can anything survive in a dry, scorching desert? Amazingly, there are many plants that can, from tiny "living stones" the size of pebbles to giant cacti three times taller than a giraffe.

Plants need to be tough to survive in the desert. They have to deal with daytime temperatures that soar above 30°C (86°F) and nighttime temperatures that plunge to freezing or below. Then they have to find water—and hang on to it. Finally, they have to protect themselves from hungry animals. To cope with these challenges, desert plants use all kinds of clever tricks.

Keeping Cool

Plants elsewhere gather as much of the Sun's energy as they possibly can, but desert plants are bathed in more sunlight than they can use. Lots of people wear light-colored clothes in summer. That's because light colors reflect the Sun's rays and so help keep you cool. Desert plants use the same method. Many of them are pale green or silvery gray, while the quiver tree of the Namib and Kalahari deserts of southern Africa grows branches that are covered in a chalky white powder.

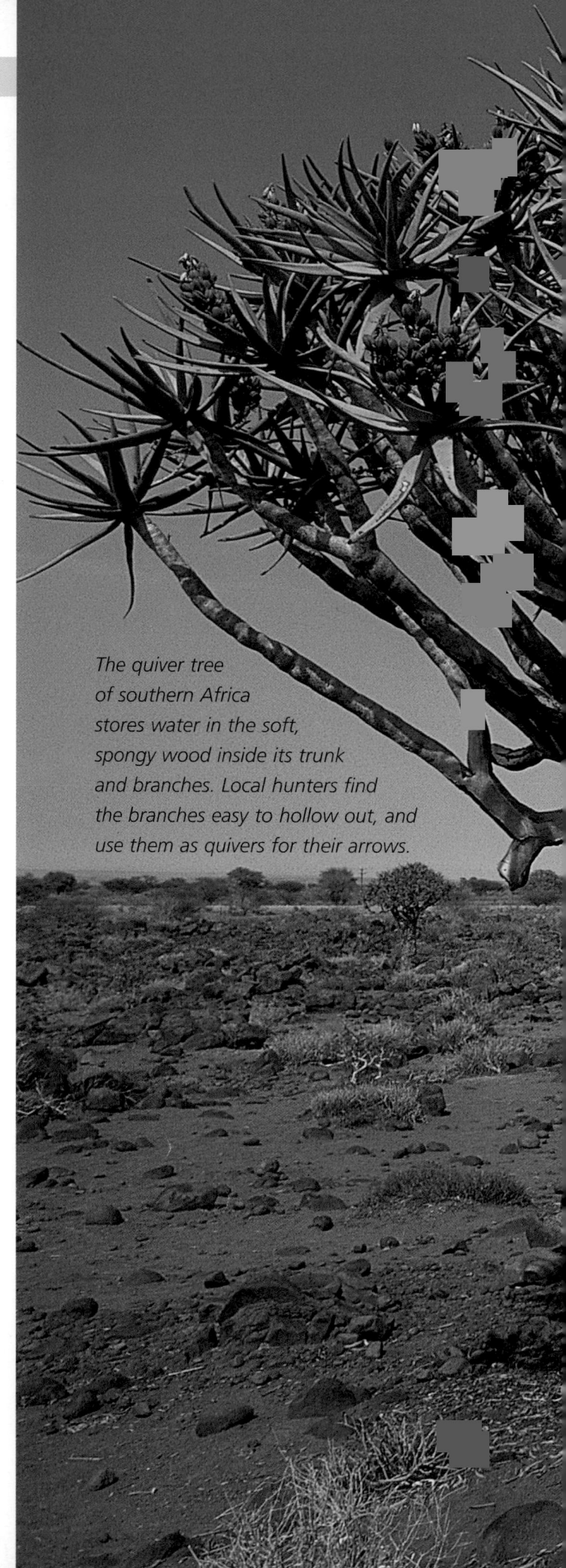

The quiver tree of southern Africa stores water in the soft, spongy wood inside its trunk and branches. Local hunters find the branches easy to hollow out, and use them as quivers for their arrows.

Old-Timers

Strangely enough, deserts are home to some of the longest-living plants in the world.

▲ Some bristlecone pines growing on the dry slopes of California's White Mountains are around 5,000 years old. This means that they were already 500 years old when the ancient Egyptians built the great pyramids. The tallest of these trees are only 15 meters (50 feet) high—but it might have taken them 3,000 years to reach this height.

▲ The creosote bush, which also grows in the deserts of California, sends out roots in all directions. From these roots grow a circle of clones (identical copies) of the original plant. Scientists calculate from the size of one circle that the original plant was alive nearly 12,000 years ago, when prehistoric people first started to grow crops.

▲ *Welwitschia* plants like the one below in the Namib Desert of southern Africa can live for up to 2,000 years. Some started growing when the Roman Empire was at the peak of its power.

Getting a Drink

Plants get most of the water they need through their roots. Because there is little water to be found in deserts, the plants that grow there need to send their roots very deep

The saguaro cactus, like many other cacti, has a ribbed surface. This allows it to expand like a concertina to absorb water.

to get as much water as possible. While deserts may be quite dry at the surface for most of the time, there is often water deep underground. To get at this water, some desert plants have a long, thick central root, called a taproot. The taproot of the mesquite tree, which grows in the American Southwest, can pierce down 15 meters (50 feet)—the height of a five-story building. The root of the camelthorn **acacia** tree of Africa can reach down twice as far.

Another way that a plant can collect scarce water is to spread its roots over a broad area, and this is exactly what many cacti do. They send out a wide net of hairlike roots in all directions, just below the surface. When it rains, the network of roots collects the water before it seeps deeper into the ground. The same roots can even absorb the dew that sometimes forms in deserts overnight.

Water from Thin Air

Other desert plants take in water through their leaves. One such plant is the bizarre *Welwitschia* of the Namib Desert in southwestern Africa. The *Welwitschia* is a low-growing plant with long, tattered, straplike leaves. These leaves can take in tiny droplets of water from the sea fogs that roll in from the Atlantic Ocean in the early morning—about the only regular source of water in the Namib.

The Welwitschia might look like a ragged mess, but it's a survivor. Many Welwitschia plants have lived for 500–600 years in the Namib, which is one of the world's driest deserts, and some have lived much longer.

Storing Water

Getting hold of water is only half the battle—desert plants also have to store it somewhere, because there might not be any more water around for a very long time. Some kinds of plants are particularly good at storing water inside themselves. These plants are called **succulents**, which means juicy. The succulents include the cacti and agaves of the Americas and the euphorbias of Africa and Asia. Agaves have thick, fleshy, sword-shaped leaves spiking outward from the center of the plant. Euphorbias come in all shapes and sizes, from little herbs called spurges to spine-covered trees.

When it rains, cacti suck in huge amounts of water and swell up like balloons. The organ-pipe cactus, which grows three times taller than a man, can hold more than 380 liters (100 gallons) in its stem—enough to fill six bathtubs. This reservoir can see the cactus through four months of drought.

Plants don't have to be big to be good at surviving dry periods. For example, the wild tulips of the deserts of Central Asia live through most of the year as small underground bulbs. When the spring rains come, the bulbs quickly send up leaves and flowers. These die back at the start of the long summer, but the bulbs store enough food and water to last

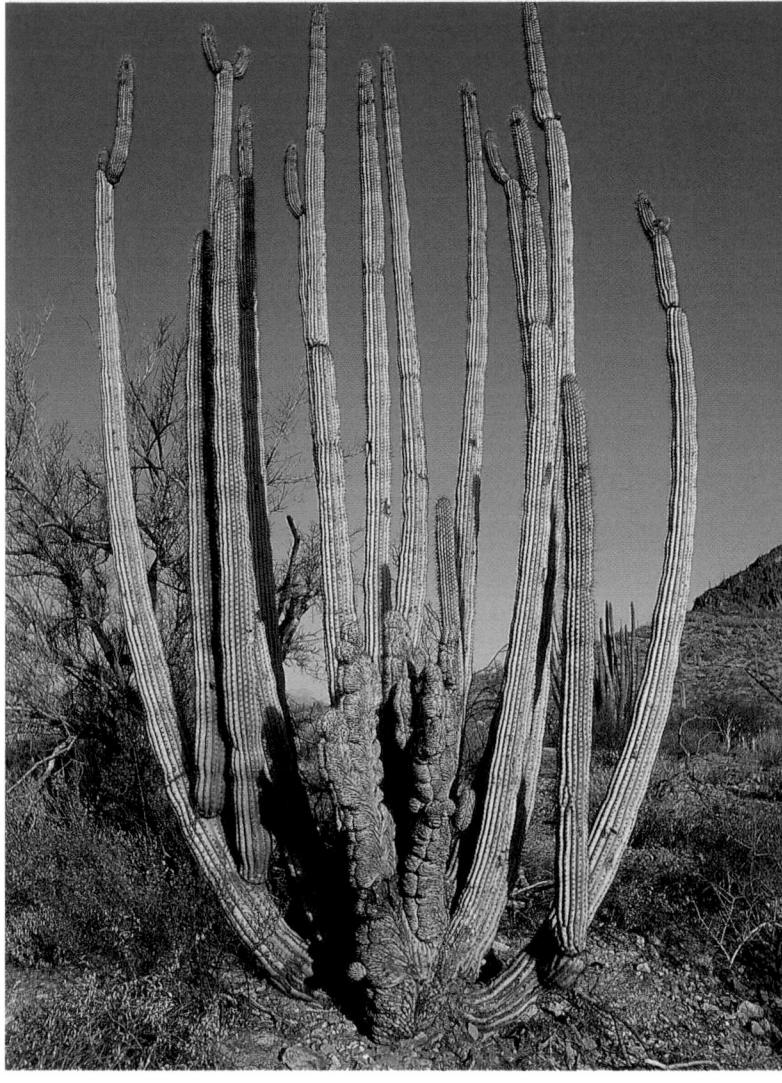

Like the saguaro cactus, the organ-pipe cactus is typical of the Sonoran Desert of Arizona and Mexico.

 Homes in the Desert

Although there are hardly any trees in the deserts of the American Southwest, the giant saguaro cacti are the next best thing as far as birds are concerned. The cacti have places for birds like the red-tailed hawk to nest, and Gila woodpeckers (left) and elf owls nest in holes in the great stem. The camelthorn acacia tree of southern Africa also makes a home for many animals, including acacia rats and bush babies (galagos).

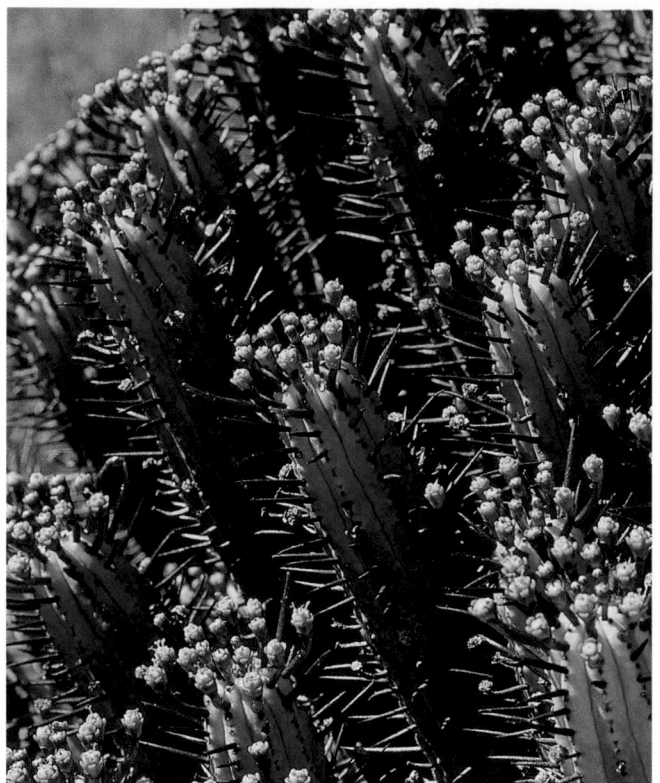

Left: Many species of euphorbias live in African deserts. They are not cacti, but look just like cacti because they have thick, juicy stems that store water, and because they protect themselves with spines.

up more water from the ground, bringing up other useful chemicals with it. However, in the fiercely hot conditions of the desert, water evaporates from leaves too easily, and there's very little water in the ground to replace it. Most plants would quickly shrivel up and die, but desert plants have ways to stop this from happening.

Looking at a spiny cactus, you might think, "That's a strange plant. It doesn't have any leaves." Only spines emerge from its thick, fleshy stem. Cacti have lost their leaves and replaced them with small spikes that do not lose water. Instead of making food in leaves, they make food in the green stem, where there are far fewer pores.

In the Kara-Kum desert of Central Asia, the black saxaul tree uses an alternative method. For most of the year it has no leaves

until the next spring. The tulips that people grow in their gardens are all descended from these tough little desert survivors.

Preventing Water Loss

Once a plant has built up a good store of water, it needs to hang on to it. But no plant can avoid losing some water—it's part of the way they keep themselves alive.

All plants give off water vapor into the air. Most of the water vapor escapes through tiny pores (holes) in the leaves, which plants have to keep open to survive. The pores serve to take in **carbon dioxide**, a vital gas that they use to make food. So, to get carbon dioxide, plants have to lose a bit of water. Losing water can sometimes help them, though, because it makes their roots suck

Right: Tulips, like this one growing in eastern Turkey, were taken to Belgium and Holland in the 16th century, starting the tulip-growing industry. They were so popular that some people made a fortune selling them.

Beckoning Branches

Mormons named this desert plant the Joshua tree because they imagined its branches were the arms of the Hebrew leader Joshua beckoning them to the promised land. The Joshua tree is the largest type of yucca plant, and it lives in the Mojave Desert, where it has to cope with thin, rocky soil and extremely hot, dry weather. These conditions might seem inhospitable to us, but Joshua trees seem to like them—they live nowhere else.

Desert Plants of North America

The different deserts of the American Southwest look distinctive because they have different species of plants. People can recognize parts of the Sonoran Desert, for example, because they are full of saguaro cacti, while the characteristic look of the Mojave Desert is due to the abundant Joshua trees.

Joshua tree. Typical of the Mojave Desert.

Saguaro cactus. Typical of the Sonoran Desert.

Big sagebrush. Common in the Great Basin.

Soaptree yucca. Grows in the Sonoran and Chihuahuan deserts.

Ponderosa pine. Lives in the mountains between the deserts.

Boojum tree. Common in Baja California.

Creosote bush. Widespread throughout the Southwest.

and makes food instead in its whitish-green twigs and branches. Once the tree has flowered, borne fruit, and spread its seeds, it often sheds some of its branches to cut down evaporation even more.

Cacti, like the other succulent plants, only open their pores to take in carbon dioxide at night, when it's a lot cooler. At these low temperatures, very little water can evaporate.

Tubby Plants

Many cacti have a shape that helps reduce water loss. You might think that all cacti are the tall, thin giants you see in cowboy movies, but most of them are small and squat and round. Spherical (round) shapes have a small surface area compared to their size. Since it's from the surface of plants that water evaporates, spherical cacti have the smallest possible surface area from which they can lose water. At the same time, they contain the greatest space for water storage. Desert grasses also tend to have shapes that help them cut down on water loss. For example, esparto grass, which grows on the northern edge of the Sahara, has rolled-up leaves. Most of its pores are on the inside surface of the rolled leaf, so rolling shades its pores from the Sun. In the semidesert areas of southwest Asia, the spear grasses lay their leaves out flat when it rains, but roll them up when it gets hot and dry again.

Desert plants sometimes use chemicals as well as shape to stop them from losing water. Euphorbias have stems filled with a white, sticky, poisonous liquid that does not evaporate easily. Many desert plants ooze poisonous chemicals into the ground around them. This stops other plants from growing nearby and tapping into their water supplies. Other desert plants send out a dense mat of roots that stops other young plants from growing nearby. This is why plants in deserts are often spaced very regularly.

Desert Feasts

In the deserts of the United States and Mexico, people eat some types of agaves. The leaves of agaves are tough, sword-shaped, and spiky, but the stem and flowers of some types are delicious roasted, boiled, or scrambled with eggs. In southern Africa, the local people have found all sorts of plant food in the Kalahari Desert. They get starch (a source of sugar) from some corms and tubers (swollen roots), and protein from foods such as mongongo nuts and tsin beans. The fruits of the marula tree (related to the mango) and the bottle-shaped baobab tree are both full of vitamin C. The Kalahari is also home to the wild watermelon (below), which quenches the thirst of both people and animals.

Self-Defense

In the deserts of the American Southwest, the chemicals in the sagebrush not only poison the ground around it but also give the plant a revolting taste. Being poisonous is one sure way that a plant can protect itself from being eaten.

Another well-known example of chemical defense is the creosote bush. Its leaves contain a poisonous oil that smells

The stumpy, rounded shape of these living stones makes them look like small pebbles—useful for camouflage, but also good for preventing water loss.

like creosote, the foul-smelling chemical that people use to preserve timber.

Desert plants also have more visible defenses. Cacti, agaves, and desert euphorbias are all armed with sharp spines. Some cacti, such as the cholla of American deserts, also have barbed bristles, while a large variety of desert trees and shrubs, such as acacias, are covered in vicious thorns. The milkweed plant of southwest Asia has long ribs between its leaves. When the ribs die they become hard and sharp, forming a kind of spiky cage around the flowers. Milkweed also grows very

The creosote bush has a foul taste that repels almost all desert animals. The creosote bush grasshopper is the only known animal that eats the plant's leaves.

close to the ground, which makes it more difficult for animals to eat.

One desert plant makes itself even more difficult to eat by hiding underground. This is the window plant of the Namib Desert, which buries its plump, upright leaves under the surface. Only the tips of the leaves appear above the surface. These tips—the "windows"—are made of a see-through material that lets sunlight reach the rest of the leaves below ground. Burying its leaves underground also helps the window plant cut down on water loss.

The next best thing to staying completely out of sight is to use a disguise. The living stones of the Namib Desert look just like pebbles. Only when you peer at them very closely can you see that the round stone is made up of two mottled, fleshy lumps that are in fact leaves. From a distance, people can recognize a living stone as a plant only when it flowers—but the flowers, although wonderfully bright and colorful to attract insects, last only for a couple of days.

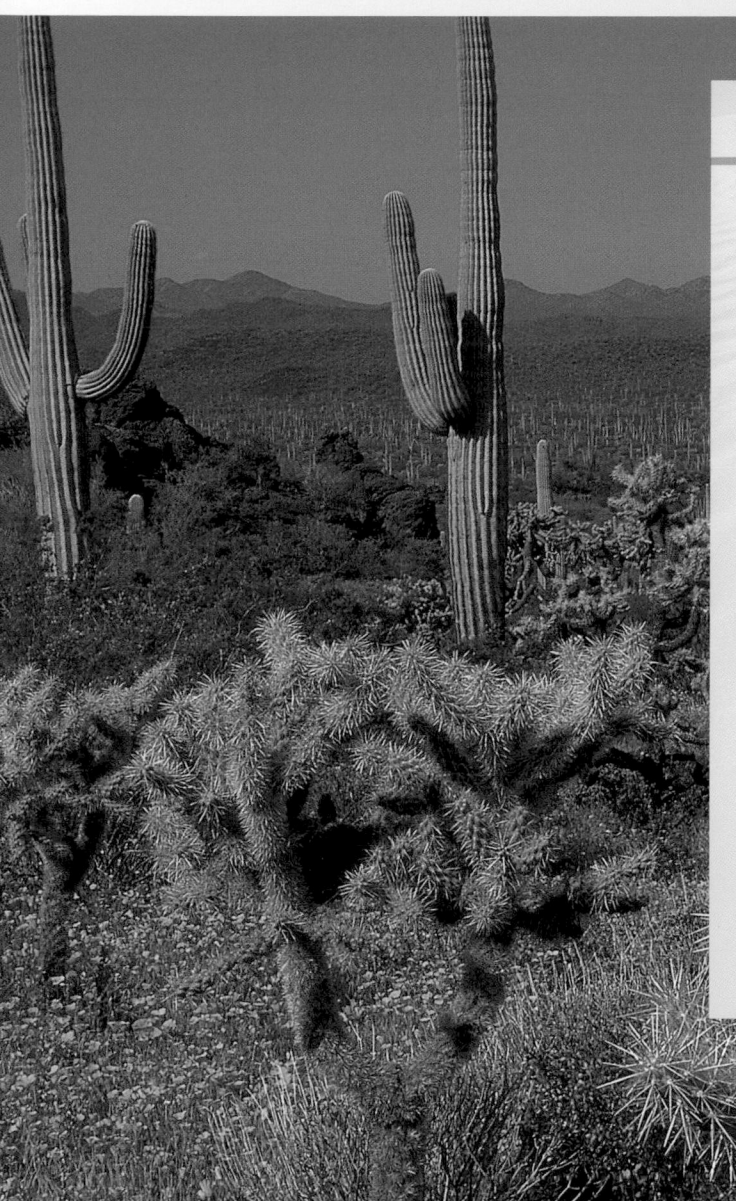

Cactus Facts

▲ There are more than 1,600 species of cacti. They live on the American continents, all the way from Canada to Argentina.

▲ The smallest cactus is about 1 centimeter (0.5 inches) across. The largest is the saguaro cactus, which can grow as tall as 18 meters (60 feet).

▲ Large cacti can take in 800 liters (210 gallons) of water at one time when it rains.

▲ A saguaro cactus 6 meters (20 feet) tall can hold more than a tonne (1 ton) of water in its stem.

▲ Many wild cacti are protected by law. However, the removal of young saguaros by "plant poachers" is a problem. The poachers sell the slow-growing cacti for about $60 per 30 centimeters (1 foot) to plant collectors. Poachers caught in Arizona are given a heavy fine or even a jail sentence.

The Blooming Desert

We don't normally think of deserts as colorful places, but in the Sonoran Desert in Arizona and Mexico, millions of flowers sometimes appear together in spring, after winter rainstorms. They are "ephemerals"— plants whose life cycle lasts a matter of days. For most of the time only their seeds are present, lying dormant (inactive) in the soil. After heavy rain, they sprout, burst into flower, and quickly produce more seeds before the ground dries out. Then they shrivel up and die. Desert ephemerals include poppies, daisies, and members of the pea family. The seeds can survive years waiting for rain, but they take as little as two hours to produce leaves once they get soaked.

KALAHARI AND NAMIB

The Kalahari stretches across Botswana, while the red sands of the Namib run down the coast of Namibia into South Africa. The Kalahari is not the driest of deserts, but the Namib has so little water that its plants and animals must rely on fog.

 Fact File

▲ The Skeleton Coast in the Namib Desert is one of the world's driest places. Some people think it is named for the remains of shipwrecked sailors who died there before finding water.

▲ The Okavango River is overwhelmed by the sandy dryness of the Kalahari and peters out into a swampy wetland, the Okavango Delta.

▲ On the Namib coast, jackass, or little, penguins dig nesting burrows in the guano (hardened deposits of bird droppings) from millions of other seabirds. Collection of guano by humans to use as fertilizer has reduced the numbers of jackass penguins.

 Collecting Fog

There is hardly any rain in the Namib, but there is a cold-water current in the nearby Atlantic Ocean. The cold water creates fog, which rolls in from the ocean on most mornings. Any moisture available to plants and animals comes in the form of this fog. Some Namib beetles have a cunning way of getting a drink. In the early morning, the beetles stand on the sand with their back ends raised in the air and catch fog droplets on their bodies. The tiny drops of water then join and trickle down toward the beetles' mouths.

A fog bank shows the immense height of the sand dunes on the Namib coast, some of which rise to 300 meters (1,000 feet).

1. Skeleton Coast
This stretch of desolate, extremely arid coast is now a national park.

2. Walvis Bay
Millions of Cape fur seals and seabirds breed here on the desert coast. They feed in the rich fishing grounds offshore.

3. Sossusvlei
One of many pans: shallow depressions in the land that flood after heavy rains. Nearby, sand dunes 300 meters (1,000 feet) tall are called "sand mountains."

4. Diamond Mines
Deposits of diamonds lie under the sands of the Namib. Off-road driving for mining exploration is damaging the wildlife.

5. Etosha Pan
When flooded, this large, shallow depression attracts hordes of animals. Pesticides and poaching threaten wildlife.

6. Dry Rivers
The Kalahari has virtually no surface water. Its rivers have dry beds most of the time and flow only in unusually wet months.

7. Okavango Delta
The water here attracts elephants, lions, wildebeest, and zebras. There are plans to build a hydro-electric powerstation, which would cause habitat loss.

8. CKGR
The Central Kalahari Game Reserve (CKGR) protects the traditional lifestyle of the San people. Poaching threatens the wildlife.

9. Makgadikgadi Salt Pans
The pans fill with water when the Okavango Delta overflows during wet weather.

31

DESERT ANIMALS

We often think of deserts as empty places, where no animals live. In fact, a great variety of animals are at home in deserts, from tiny insects to large mammals like antelope and camels. There are even elephants living in deserts.

All land animals depend on plants for food. Either they eat plants themselves, or they eat other animals that feed on plants. In the driest deserts there are hardly any plants, so plant-eating animals can survive only by eating seeds or other bits of plants blown into the desert by the wind. Such food is enough only for very small animals, like insects. Spiders, snakes, and lizards eat the insects, and they, in turn, are eaten by larger animals, such as birds of prey.

Wetter deserts have a wider range of plants, including grasses, cacti, shrubs, or even scattered trees. Deserts that are rich in plant life provide enough food for larger animals, such as rabbits, antelope, camels, and—in Australia—kangaroos. In Africa, herds of antelope travel huge distances to find enough plants to keep them alive, and predators such as lions and leopards often follow them into the desert in the hope of an easy meal. Other desert hunters include

There is hardly anything to eat on the dunes of the Namib Desert in southern Africa. Oryx, a kind of antelope, survive there by drinking at the water holes and eating the sparse plants on the plains.

coyotes and foxes in the deserts of North America, and pumas in the cold Patagonian desert of South America.

Most desert animals can't afford to be too fussy about what they eat, but some have very particular requirements. The yucca moth, for example, depends entirely on yucca plants for its survival—and yucca plants depend just as much on the moth.

Yuccas are plants with a rosette of long, sharp-tipped leaves surrounding a flower stalk in the middle. The female yucca moth lays her eggs in the middle of a yucca flower, and the caterpillars that hatch feed on a few of the developing seeds inside the flower. To make sure the flower will make seeds, the moth first collects a ball of pollen from a different yucca flower, and then rubs this on her chosen flower after laying the eggs. No other insect can pollinate the yucca flower, and no other flower provides a suitable home for the caterpillars—so yuccas and yucca moths depend on each other to survive.

Another specialist feeder is the gerenuk, a long-necked gazelle that lives in the deserts of Somalia in east Africa (*gerenuk* means "giraffe-necked" in the Somali language). The gerenuk feeds on the leaves of thorny bushes. By standing on its hind legs and stretching its long neck, it can reach much higher leaves than other animals can.

Threatened Animals

Many desert and semidesert animals are under the threat of extinction. They include the Asiatic wild ass, the Arabian oryx, the houbara bustard—all from Asia —the African penguin (which breeds on the margins of semidesert areas), and the American desert tortoise. There are various reasons why they are threatened. Loss of habitat to farmland and expanding cities is probably the main reason. Hunting and the pet trade are also to blame for the disappearance of animals. In some regions, wildlife has to compete with livestock for grazing. Introduced predators have had a devastating effect on wild animals. In Australia, cats and foxes have severely reduced the numbers of many native desert animals. Climate change and global warming are affecting many species, especially amphibians. In addition, warmer temperatures are resulting in more wildfires in arid regions.

Conservation involves protecting wild areas, making it illegal to hunt or kill wild animals, and in some cases running breeding programs in zoos and reserves with the hope of reintroducing captive animals into the wild. For example, Asiatic wild asses have been successfully reintroduced into the Negev Desert in Israel. The scimitar-horned oryx of northern Africa was hunted to extinction in the wild in the 20th century. Since the 1960s, zoos and reserves have run breeding programs for this antelope and there are now several thousand oryx around the world. And there is hope that soon some of these captive oryx will be released back into semidesert in Tunisia, northern Africa.

Many types of scorpions, such as this bark scorpion of California, have made deserts their own. In some places there is a greater total weight of scorpions than any other animals except ants and termites.

energy from food. Some desert rodents get nearly all their water this way. Other desert animals can go without drinking for a long time. Camels can survive for a week without drinking when they are working, and for several months when they're not. When they do drink, they can take in over 100 liters (26 gallons) in one session. People often think that camels store water in their humps, but the humps are full of fatty tissue. Camels use this as a sort of emergency food supply, and it can be broken down inside the camel's body to release water.

Finding water is not easy in the desert. Large desert animals like antelope travel long distances to get to water holes, where they can drink. Some antelope, as well as wild horses and asses, are good at breaking up the dry ground with their hooves to get at small

Finding Water

Like a number of other desert animals, the gerenuk never has to drink—it gets all the water it needs from the leaves it eats. In fact, all animals can make water inside their bodies by a chemical reaction. This water comes from the chemical process that releases

Desert Makers

Animals can help make deserts. During the time of the ancient Romans, parts of North Africa were much greener than today, and the Romans built cities (right) and even grew wheat in the region. After the fall of the Roman Empire, the complicated irrigation systems that watered the crops fell into ruin. Rather than growing wheat, people took to raising sheep and goats. If there are too many sheep and goats in an area, the animals strip the vegetation—grass, shrubs, trees, everything. They also eat any new shoots that appear, so there is no chance for plants to recover. This process, called overgrazing, can turn fertile land into a desert. Even today, the Sahara is expanding southward every year because of overgrazing and slash-and-burn farming.

amounts of water under the surface. The thorny devil, a spiky lizard from Australia, has scales on its body that can soak up water from damp sand.

It's important for desert animals not to lose water. Animals lose water when they urinate, but they have to urinate to get rid of waste products in the body. This process is called **excretion**. To reduce water loss, camels and other desert animals have very concentrated urine; in other words, their urine contains only a small amount of water, which makes it particularly dark and smelly. Some desert reptiles excrete solid crystals instead of liquid urine. Other reptiles get rid of certain waste products, such as salts, through glands on the sides of their snouts.

Wasting Nothing

Animals also lose water in their droppings, so most desert animals have very dry droppings. Camel dung is incredibly dry and solid—for thousands of years desert people have used it as a fuel instead of firewood, which is hard to find in the desert. North American kangaroo rats make sure they don't waste any water in their droppings by eating them.

Another way animals lose water is by sweating. Sweating is a way of keeping cool, but camels can stand being warmer than most other mammals before they need to start sweating. They have fewer sweat glands than other animals, and their thick coat keeps the scorching sunlight off their skin, which stops them from getting too hot.

One Hump or Two?

There are two kinds of camels. The Arabian camel (also called a dromedary, below) has one hump. It lives in North Africa and southwest Asia. It is now a domestic animal, although some of the camels introduced to Australia in the 19th century have become wild. The other kind of camel is the two-humped Bactrian camel, which lives in Central Asia. Most Bactrian camels are also domesticated (bred), but there are still a few wild herds in remote parts of Mongolia and western China. Camels are sometimes called ships of the desert because they are so good at carrying goods and people across seas of sand. They can keep going for a long time without food or water, and have many other ways of dealing with life in the desert. For example, camels have a web of skin joining the two toes on each foot. This web spreads out as they walk, keeping the foot from sinking into soft sand. It's a bit like wearing snowshoes. When the wind blows sand in their faces, camels can close their nostrils. They also have long, thick eyelashes that protect their eyes from sand.

Above: Sand in desert dunes is so loose that animals can swim through it. Some small geckos even have webbed feet, like a frog's feet, to help them swim.

Surviving Heat and Cold

Many deserts are very hot during the day, but at night the temperature can plummet to freezing.

To avoid the heat of the day, small desert animals often shelter under rocks or dig burrows. Some animals only come out at night, when it's cooler. Nighttime hunters include the fennec (a fox of North Africa) and the western diamondback rattlesnake of the American Southwest. The western diamondback has little pits beneath its eyes that can detect infrared radiation (heat). This helps it "see" its prey—usually warm-blooded rodents—in the dark.

Sometimes it gets too cold to go out at night. Animals like the kangaroo rat of North America and the mouselike jerboa of Asia and North Africa come out of their shelters mainly at dawn and dusk, when the temperature is most comfortable.

Ears that Radiate

Jerboas, which are also called desert rats, have very long hind legs that enable them to hop along quickly. They also have big ears. Other desert mammals, like the fennec and the similar kit fox of the American Southwest, have big ears, too. A big, flat ear is like a radiator. There is very little volume and a lot of surface area to give off (radiate) heat. So big ears help lose heat from the animal's body and keep the animal cool.

Most birds have a higher body temperature than mammals. Nevertheless, the intense desert sunshine would cause them to overheat unless they had some method of cooling off.

This round-tailed ground squirrel lives in the American deserts. It gets all the water it needs from its food, but it needs food rich in water, such as this cactus flower.

Not all oryx make it in the harsh environment of the Namib Desert. The remains of this one might have been scavenged by jackals and hyenas, which range widely across the dunes.

RUSSIA

KAZAKHSTAN

Aral
Sea

Caspian Sea

GEORGIA

ARMENIA

AZERBAIJAN

TURKEY

SYRIA

IRAQ

KUWAIT

SAUDI ARABIA

BAHRAIN

QATAR

UAE   OMAN

Persian Gulf

TURKMENISTAN

UZBEKISTAN

KYRGYZSTAN

TAJIKISTAN

AFGHANISTAN

IRAN

PAKISTAN

NEPAL

INDIA

TIBET

BHUTAN

BANGLADESH

MYANM
(BURM

0   500 miles
0   500   kilometers

Desert Animals of Asia

The deserts of central Asia are barren. The sparse rains support few plants, so the food supply for animals is meager. Plant-eating mammals such as the wild ass, Bactrian camel, and Mongolian gazelle travel widely to find enough grazing. Even outside the migrating season, gazelles cover more than 20 kilometers (12 miles) per day in their endless search for food.

Meat eaters in the desert must make the most of each rare opportunity to feed. So while the corsac fox and the steppe eagle hunt desert rodents, they also survive by scavenging carcasses whenever they can.

The houbara bustard is also a flexible feeder and has a wide taste in food. It collects seeds and shoots but also preys on locusts, beetles, and lizards when it finds them.

Asiatic wild ass

Bactrian camel

Steppe eagle

Mongolian gazelle

Houbara bustard

Corsac fox

Many desert birds have a way of fanning themselves to keep cool: they flutter a patch of skin on their throats.

Sunbathing Reptiles

Birds and mammals are sometimes called **warm-blooded** because their bodies are always at the same warm temperature. They use a lot of energy in keeping their bodies at the right temperature, and all this energy comes from their food. In fact, they use about 90 percent of the food they eat to keep their body temperature steady.

Cold-blooded animals, such as snakes and lizards, don't need to keep their bodies at a steady temperature. They can spend most of their time cold and inactive, using very little energy. Because of this, reptiles can get by on a tenth of the food that mammals and birds need. This gives snakes and lizards an advantage in deserts, where food is scarce.

Cold-blooded isn't a very good description, because a reptile's body temperature changes with that of its surroundings. Its body is colder than a mammal's at night, but at midday in the desert it might be warmer.

A viper can detect its prey with heat-sensitive pits on its snout. These pits are so sophisticated that they work like a second pair of eyes, forming a picture of the victim's body heat.

When a desert lizard wakes up in the morning, its body is cool. Its body processes, including the movement of its muscles, work slowly. The lizard can only move sluggishly, but once it has crawled from its shelter and into the Sun, it begins to warm up. Moving slowly is one disadvantage of being cold-blooded, especially if a warm-blooded predator is on the prowl. When the lizard is warm, its muscles work quickly enough for it to scuttle about looking for food, or escaping from birds of prey. As the air gets hotter, desert lizards often climb to the higher branches of a bush, where there is more breeze to cool them. By midday, when the Sun is at its hottest, the lizard might look for shade under a rock.

Being cold-blooded has other advantages in the desert. Animals lose water as they breathe, but cold-blooded animals only need

The Arabian jerboa is one of the many desert rodents that scrape out a living scurrying beneath the thin desert soil by day, coming out to steal seeds at night.

to breathe very, very slowly when they are resting. As a result, reptiles lose much less water than birds or mammals. And while mammals have to sweat to cool themselves in hot weather, cold-blooded animals simply let their bodies heat up. This allows reptiles to survive on much less water than mammals or birds, making them expert desert dwellers.

Staying Out of the Heat

Some desert animals, like spiders and scorpions, avoid the problems of heat and lack of water by becoming **dormant**. When an animal is dormant, it stays completely inactive—sometimes for weeks or months on end. It neither eats nor moves, and appears so lifeless that it seems to be dead. Dormant animals wake up only when there is a chance of eating something, or of mating. In the Sahara, desert snails can remain dormant for years until brought back to life by rain. In Australia, various kinds of tiny shrimps lie dormant in the desert. The wind blows their eggs until they settle in a crevice or a hollow in rock, and the eggs stay there until it rains. When the hollow fills up with water, the eggs hatch. Such shrimps have even been found in hollows high up on the sunbaked sides of Uluru (Ayers Rock), the famous giant rock in the middle of the Australian desert.

Some birds search for food in the desert, but they build their nests in more comfortable places beyond the

The Australian desert pool where these shield shrimps live is drying up. But when it forms again with the next rains, the shrimps' eggs are ready to hatch and grow, before any other pond creatures arrive in the pool.

edge of the desert, such as forests, mountains, or grasslands. This is no problem for birds like eagles and vultures, which can fly great distances with little effort. These birds also have incredibly sharp vision and can spot an animal on the ground from a long way off. By roaming vast areas, such birds can find just enough food for themselves and their distant chicks back at the nest.

The strange duckbill of the shovelnosed lizard helps it burrow in the loose sand of the Namib Desert. It can quickly plunge in to extract prey such as this fly.

Life on the Dunes

Sand dunes are a unique and challenging habitat for both plants and animals. The sand is always blowing about in the wind, making it difficult for any plants to grow. Nevertheless, a great variety of small animals live there. For example, the huntsman spider (inset) makes its home in a tunnel in the sand. It lines the tunnel with silk and makes a trapdoor at the entrance to keep out windblown sand.

Lying in wait for larger prey is the sidewinding adder (below). This small snake shuffles completely into the fine sand of the Namib Desert. It leaves only its eyes exposed, and the tip of its tail, which it waves to attract lizards near enough to catch.

SAHARA

The Sahara stretches across North Africa, from the Atlantic Ocean to the Red Sea. It is the largest desert and covers one-twelfth of Earth's land surface.

 ## Desert Mammals

Mammals in the Sahara avoid the scorching heat by staying underground during the day. The fennec, a kind of fox, hides out in its burrows in large family groups. Nevertheless, to survive in the Sahara, it must have the ability to go without a drink for long periods. At night the fennec comes out to hunt small rodents, lizards, and insects such as locusts. Its densely furred feet allow it to run fast on loose sand, and it can keep cool by losing body heat through its huge ears.

 ## Sahara Facts

▲ The Sahara covers parts of 11 countries: Morocco, Algeria, Tunisia, Libya, Egypt, Western Sahara, Mauritania, Mali, Niger, Chad, and Sudan.

▲ The Sahara is expanding southward because of overgrazing by livestock and poor farming techniques.

▲ Few people live in the Sahara. On average there is less than one person per square kilometer (0.4 square miles)—the same as Alaska.

Lake Nasser was formed when the Aswan Dam was built on the Nile River. The dammed water is used to irrigate fields and generate electricity.

1. Disputed Territory
Both Morocco and Mauritania have made claims for the region called Western Sahara. The area used to be administered by Spain. Conflict in the region threatens wildlife.

2. Atlas Mountains
Stretching across northern Algeria and Morocco, these mountains mark the northwestern border of the Sahara. The Atlas bear, a type of brown bear, and the Barbary lion are now extinct in the region.

3. The Great Ergs, or Sand Seas
The Sahara has varied terrain, but seas of sand dunes such as the Great Ergs cover a quarter of its area.

4. Oil Fields
The Sahara's richest oil fields occur in southern Algeria and eastern Libya. Half of Africa's known oil reserves are in Libya. The use of oil as a fuel raises atmospheric levels of the gas carbon dioxide, which increases the greenhouse effect and causes global warming.

5. Chott al Jerid
A vast, flat salt lake. The lake sometimes holds water in winter, but it dries out in summer.

6. Chad Basin
Due to climate change, arid lands and salt pans now cover much of the area once covered by the waters of Lake Chad. There has been conflict between farmers and fishers over use of the lake's waters.

7. Tibesti Mountains
At 3,415 meters (11,204 feet), Mount Koussi in the Tibesti Mountains is the highest point of land in the Sahara.

8. Al Khufra Oasis
This group of five oases covers an area the size of Israel.

9. Lake Nasser
An artificial reservoir created in 1971 by the completion of the Aswan High Dam. Its waters irrigate land to the north.

PEOPLE AND THE DESERT

Imagine living in a desert—and surviving. You would have to protect yourself against extreme temperatures. You would have to find food and water when both are in short supply. Knowing the way to the nearest water hole could be a matter of life or death.

This satellite image of electric lights on Earth at night reveals where people are most concentrated. Compare it with the map on pages 6–7, and you'll notice that many of the darkest areas are deserts. However, the deserts in the United States and Saudi Arabia contain lots of light. These countries have enough resources to build cities in the desert.

From time to time, you would also have to cope with natural events such as sandstorms and flash floods. Life can be very hard in the desert, and to survive you have to be very resourceful.

Despite such difficulties, people have lived in the desert for thousands of years. Some have been **nomadic**, traveling from place to place in search of the scarce resources available. Others have settled at oases, using these rare desert springs to grow crops or to water cattle. Some have even founded bustling cities, which thrived on passing trade.

Like desert plants and animals, desert people have learned to adapt to their harsh environment. Physically, people are not well suited to the desert. Like other mammals, we are warm-blooded, which makes coping with very high or low temperatures difficult. Being warm-blooded also means we need a steady supply of food and water. Over thousands of years, desert people have developed unique lifestyles that meet these challenges. They have gathered

What to Wear in the Desert

You might think that the best way to dress in the desert would be to wear as little as possible. Certainly, a few desert peoples, such as the San of southern Africa and the Aborigines of Australia, wore few or no clothes in the past. However, most desert dwellers wear a lot of loose-fitting clothes. These help keep the body cool by shading the skin from the scorching Sun. In the Sahara (right), a man might wear long trousers, a long, flowing upper garment, and a turban wrapped around his head.

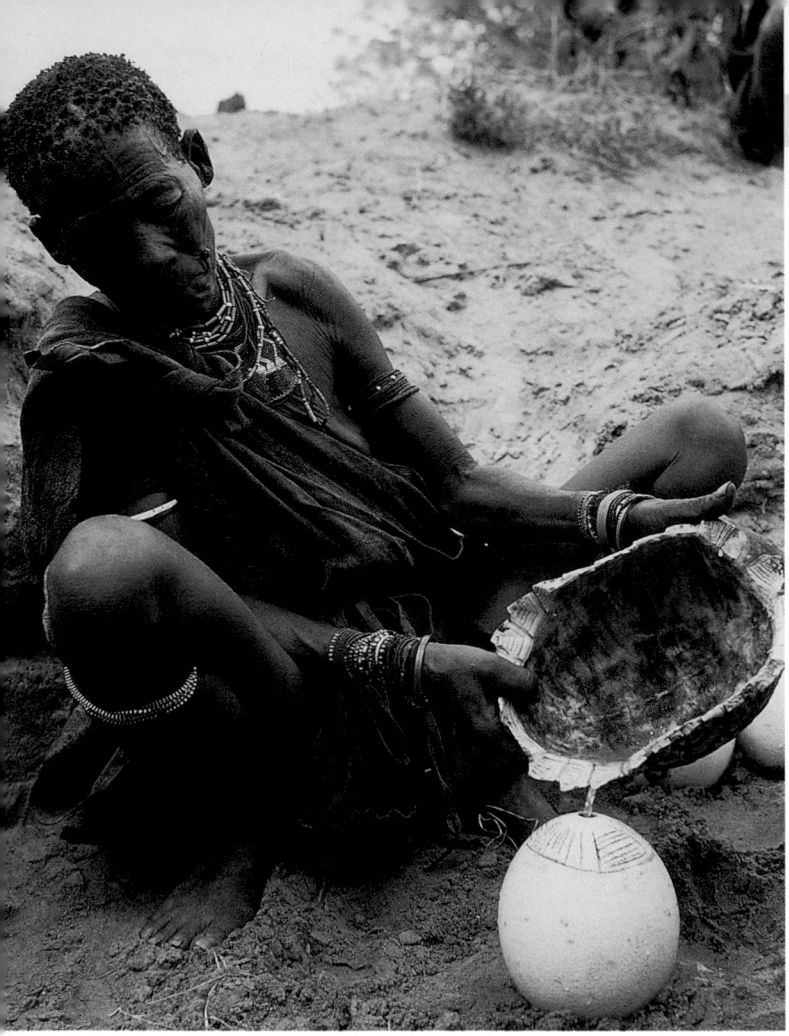

an in-depth knowledge of arid (dry) landscapes and ecology, and have learned to respect the power of the desert.

Water, Food, and Shelter

In the past, many desert people were nomads. A nomad is a person who travels frequently in search of food or water. Because there is so little water in the desert, nomads often had to travel far from one water hole or oasis to another, and they often carried a supply of water with them. The San people of the Kalahari Desert in Africa sometimes use a very unusual container to hold their water— a hollow ostrich egg. The shell of an ostrich egg is very strong and large, making a perfect flask for a long day of hunting.

The difficulty of desert life meant that everyone was kept busy. In some societies, the men went hunting while the women and children gathered fruits, roots, and other foods. Desert nomads found food and water

in the most unlikely places. An important part of the diet of the desert-dwelling Aborigines of Australia is still the witchety grub. Women and children dig up the roots of acacia bushes and cut them up to find the grubs. They eat the grubs raw or cooked in ashes. The grubs are so rich in fat, vitamins, and protein that just ten of them provide enough food for a day.

Many desert nomads were animal herders, and some people still live this way today. Such people usually herd sturdy animals, like goats and camels, which cope well with the dry climate. The animals provide leather for sandals and tents, as well as milk and, less often, meat. During the driest months, nomadic herders linger in more fertile lands close to towns and cities, but during the rainy season they move farther into the desert.

A Bedouin Welcome

Some of the best-known desert herders are the Bedouin of the Arabian, Syrian, and North African deserts. The word *bedouin* comes from an Arabic word meaning "desert dweller," and it includes many different peoples of the region. Like other nomads, the Bedouin have to carry their possessions with them, including their shelter—a light and portable tent made of goat skin or woven camel hair. The tent provides not only shade during the day but warmth at night. Bedouin tents can be very elaborate. They are often divided into two sections by a woven curtain. One section is reserved for men and for male visitors; the other is where women prepare meals and receive female guests. Bedouins treat guests with great honor, and ply them with lots of fresh, spice-flavored coffee or mint tea.

The nutritious, nutty-flavored witchety grub is the young form of a moth, so it is really a kind of caterpillar. It lives in the roots of desert acacia trees in Australia.

Finding the Way

To a stranger's eyes, a desert may look featureless and monotonous. To the eyes of a nomad, however, it is full of information—a dry riverbed, a distinctive baobab tree, or an odd-shaped rock can all help desert people find their way. In very early times, desert nomads probably made simple maps, drawn on bark or leather, that told them where to find good water or where dangers lurked. Today, Aborigines still avoid getting lost by following routes that people have used for centuries. The routes pass water holes, hunting grounds, and natural landmarks. Walkers memorize the way by learning a map chant—a kind of verbal map that is passed from generation to generation.

Until the 20th century, there were few paved roads or railroads in the world's deserts, and many desert people traveled on foot. This could be hard work, especially on rocky ground or hot, slippery sand. To protect their feet against heat and rough surfaces, some desert people wore leather sandals or shoes. However, many people, including Bedouin and Aborigines, went barefoot.

From early times, the desert people of Asia used camels both to ride on and to carry goods and possessions. Camels are very tough

Desert Civilization in the Southwest

The deserts of the southwest United States and Mexico were home to people centuries before contact with Europeans. The traces of the culture of some of these people are still visible today. The Sinagua, or Western Anasazi, for example, built multistoried cliff dwellings and developed a kind of dry farming using the sparse water available. They also used a system of irrigation to support farming in the desert. The Anasazi civilization declined in the 13th century, but the people left their buildings, such as Montezuma's Castle in Arizona (right).

The people that met the invaders from Europe and the United States in the 19th century did not live in the same way as the Sinagua. They had a range of different lifestyles, from hunting and gathering to settled agriculture.

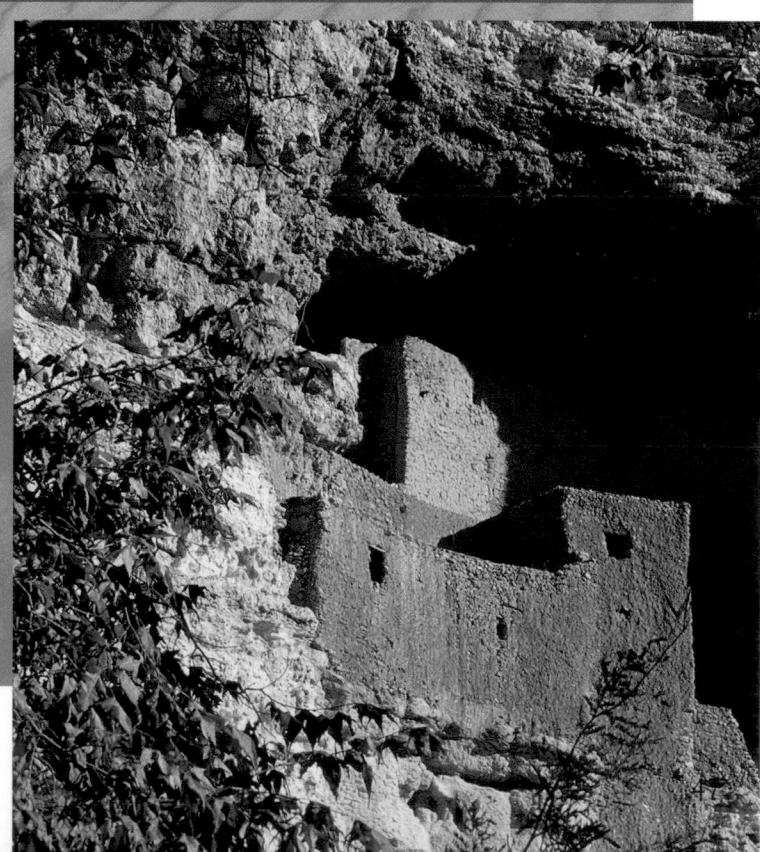

animals and can travel for days without drinking. They also provide milk, wool, and meat. Nothing is wasted. Bedouins use camel dung for fuel, and camel urine for shampoo.

Camels, Trains, and Automobiles

Camels played an especially important role in caravans. These were parties of traders or pilgrims who traveled together across the desert for safety, much like the wagon trains of the American pioneers. The largest caravans included thousands of camels. In 1908, for example, a caravan carrying salt across the Sahara numbered 20,000 camels. Caravans often moved by night to avoid walking in the daytime heat.

European explorers in Australia brought camels to the continent to help them on their long, dangerous treks across the

outback, the interior region of Australia. Robert Burke (1820/21–1861) and William Wills (1834–1861) were the first white men to cross Australia south to north, in 1861. They used 24 camels to carry their equipment, which included 20 camp beds, 80 pairs of shoes, and 30 hats. But even the camels could not survive the grueling journey. By the time Burke and Wills died of starvation and exhaustion on the return trek, all of their camels were dead, too.

The efforts of explorers like Burke and Wills helped open up the Australian outback to European settlers. In south Australia, settlers hired "cameleers" (camel drivers) from Afghanistan. The cameleers carried supplies, passengers, and mail on the long trip between Adelaide, on the south coast, and the desert settlement of Alice Springs in the center of Australia. Later, when a railroad was built between the two towns, it was named Ghan in honor of the Afghan cameleers.

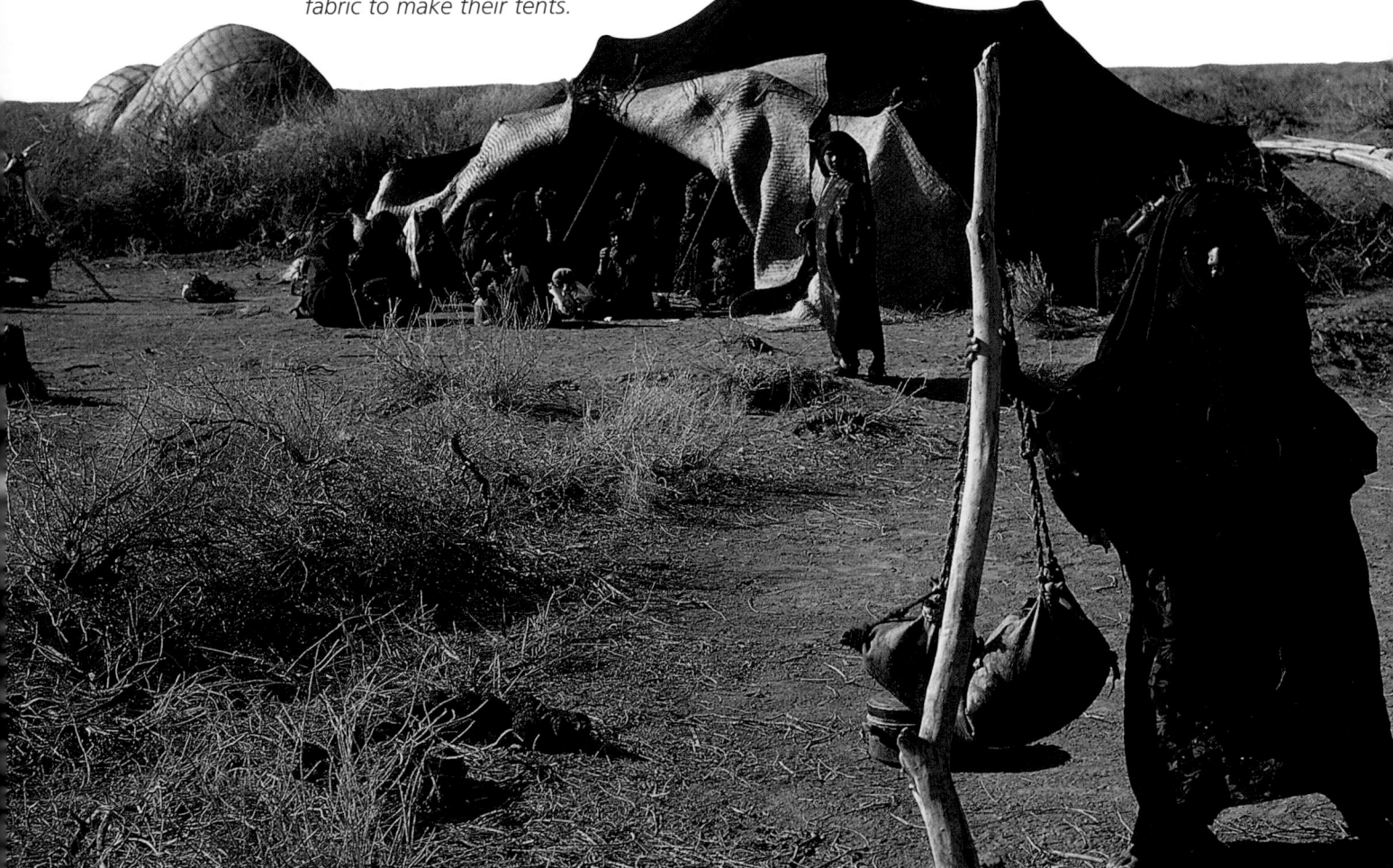

Some desert nomads rely on their animals for almost everything. These nomads in Iran use animal skins as water carriers, and weave goat hair into a lightweight fabric to make their tents.

Exploring the Arabian Desert

SAUDI ARABIA

Al Hasa oasis

Empty Quarter

OMAN

YEMEN

N

| 0 | | 300 miles |
| 0 | 300 | kilometers |

As late as 1931, twenty years after people had reached both North and South poles, there were still regions of the Arabian Desert where no European had set foot. The explorer Harry St. John Philby was already an experienced desert traveler when he finally traversed the Empty Quarter in 1932. European travelers such as Wilfred Thesiger later reported that the Empty Quarter is not quite as devoid of life as they thought. Thesiger encountered people that lived off the land even there.

—————— *Philby (1917)*
– – – – – *Philby (1918)*
••••••••• *Philby (1932)*
—————— *Thesiger (1946–1947)*
– – – – – *Thesiger (1947–1948)*

Today, even the world's most remote deserts are crossed by roads, tracks, and the occasional railroad. Many desert peoples have abandoned camels for four-wheel-drive cars. Even so, driving in the desert can be very dangerous. Wise motorists carry plenty of water in case of emergencies. On desert roads in Saudi Arabia, there are solar-powered satellite telephones beside the highways, in case an automobile breaks down.

Settling the Desert

Nomads are not the only people to have eked out a living in the desert. Since ancient times, desert people have also built permanent settlements. Many villages grew up in shady oases, where there was a reliable supply of water. Often the villagers dug deep wells to reach water trapped in layers of rock below ground. The water usually did not have to be pumped out because it sprang up naturally under its own pressure.

One of the oldest oasis settlements is the Egyptian village of Siwa, deep in the Libyan Desert. In ancient times it was the site of a temple to the Egyptian god Amon. Life at Siwa has changed very little over many centuries. The inhabitants are Berbers, an ancient people who have lived in North

⊕ Islands in the Desert

In some deserts, such as the Sahara of North Africa, there are a few places where there is always water. Such a place is called an oasis. You find oases where water from deep underground bubbles up to the surface, forming a spring. Palm trees and other plants that cannot normally survive in the desert grow around the water.

Oases are important resting places for people and camels traveling across the desert. They are also important for migrating birds, which stop at oases to drink and feed on the fruits of the trees. Some oases, such as this one in Morocco, support a lush growth of date palms and other important crops. Oases now draw tourists as well as desert people. In some areas, people are discovering that more money can be made if the oasis water is used for golf courses instead of date palms. However, the supply of water is not unlimited. One day it will run out and these areas will then become desert.

Africa for thousands of years. At Siwa, they live in mud-brick houses and make their living from the thousands of palm and olive trees that flourish in the lush oasis.

Oases can be very large, supporting a whole region of towns and villages. On the northern edge of the Empty Quarter in the southern Arabian Peninsula is the Al Hasa oasis, which covers some 120 square kilometers (47 square miles)—about the size of Boston. Its 3 million palm trees are watered by more than 60 springs. After the discovery of oil fields in the surrounding region in the 1930s, Al Hasa became even more prosperous. Today, Al Hasa is connected to the Saudi capital, Riyadh, by a paved highway as well as a railroad.

The discovery of oil and other minerals beneath some desert regions has led to further settlement of the desert. Riyadh itself was once a small, walled desert town. In the years following the discovery of oil in Saudi

Arabia in 1938, the town boomed. The oil-rich Saudi kings and businessmen built luxurious palaces, mosques, hotels, and suburbs, and today the capital has a population of more than 1.3 million people.

Exploiting the Desert

Once deserts were considered good-for-nothing wildernesses. Today, many of the world's deserts—including the Sahara, the Kara-Kum, and the Arabian deserts—are known to lie over vast deposits of oil and gas. Oil pipelines crisscross these deserts, carrying oil and gas to refineries and ports. The Trans-Arabian pipeline in Saudi Arabia is one of the longest pipelines in the world, stretching 1,719 kilometers (1,068 miles) from the eastern Saudi oil fields to the Mediterranean coast in Lebanon. That's the same as the distance along the whole west coast of the United States, from San Diego to Seattle.

Highwaymen of the Sahara?

Caravans crossing the Sahara used to travel in fear of attack from a nomadic people called the Tuareg. Tuareg men carried iron lances and double-edged swords. They wrapped their heads with long scarves colored with a brilliant blue dye that rubbed off on the skin, earning them the nickname "blue men." Many Tuareg were traders themselves, or controlled and taxed the trade routes that passed through their lands. In the 1400s they elected a sultan to organize all their trading activities, including the collection of taxes and duties. At times the Tuareg took taxes by force, which gained them a reputation for being fierce highwaymen. Arab traders fostered this reputation to scare others off the profitable trade routes.

The Tuareg are still expert desert travelers, and they have many words for the different kinds of sand dunes and the fierce winds of the Sahara. The Tuareg men on the right are riding their camels through Algeria.

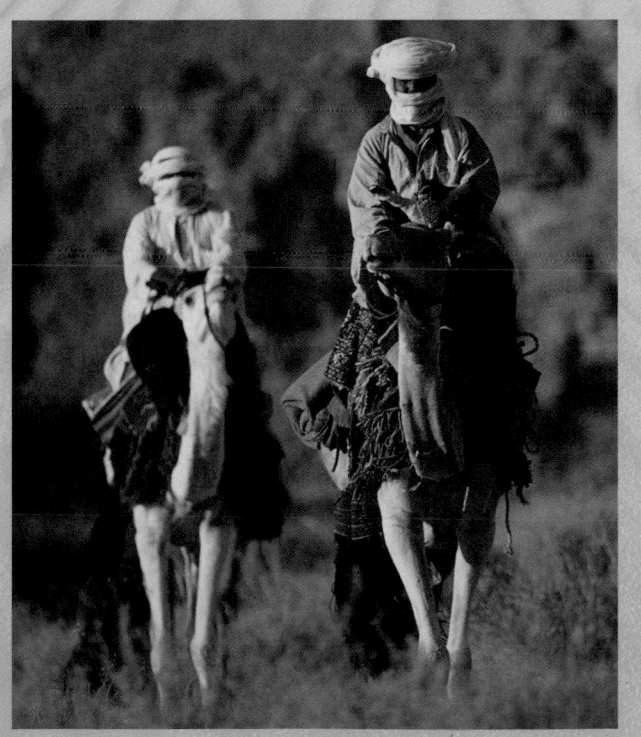

Deserts are also rich in minerals, including copper, gold, silver, phosphates, nitrates, and precious stones. For a long time, the Atacama Desert in Chile was the world's main source of nitrates, which are used to make fertilizers and explosives. In the late 19th century, the nitrates caused a war between Ecuador and Chile, who both claimed the right to the mines.

In addition to mining, some countries are carrying out expensive programs to transform barren desert lands into fertile farmland. Water for the crops is usually pumped from deep underground or carried by long pipelines from elsewhere in the country. Israel has undertaken many such projects in the arid Negev Desert in the south of the country. Supplies of water from northern Israel and a year-round abundance of sunlight help produce bumper crops of vegetables, fruits, and grains. But projects like this can sometimes damage the environment. In the 1950s, the Soviet government of Turkmenistan built the Kara-Kum Canal. The canal carried water hundreds of kilometers from the Amu Dar'ya River to the parched Kara-Kum, enabling local people to grow cotton. An unforeseen effect, however, was the shrinking of the Aral Sea, the once vast lake into which the Amu Dar'ya flows. Efforts are now being made to save a small part of the Aral Sea, called the North Aral Sea, in Kazakhstan. A dam was built in 2005, and the sea level has risen by 2 meters (7 feet).

Desert Peoples Today

Today, many nomads have abandoned the nomadic way of life and settled in cities and towns. Two-thirds of Australia's Aborigines, for example, now live in towns.

People are settling in towns for all sorts of reasons. Life in the desert can be very hard, and many desert people think their children will have better opportunities if they go to school and study, instead of learning to herd animals. Other people are simply attracted

Expanding Cities

Some of the cities located in deserts are expanding. They include Las Vegas, Nevada, in the Mojave Desert, Phoenix, Arizona, in the Sonoran Desert, and Dubai, an emirate in the Arabian Desert. This urban sprawl puts a lot of pressure on desert wildlife. For a start, animals and plants lose their habitat in the areas cleared for development. New roads and railways to the growing cities fragment habitat, which makes it more difficult for animals to find mates. And with the desert on their doorstep, more people explore it. That increases the risk of damage to the fragile desert wildlife.

One of the main requirements of people in cities is freshwater. This is a problem in deserts, where the rainfall is very low. Rivers may be diverted or canals built to bring water into cities—at a cost of depriving other regions of freshwater. In Dubai, ancient reserves of underground water are mined. But these sources cannot last forever. Dubai also removes the salt from seawater to make it suitable for drinking. However, this process—called desalination—uses a lot of energy. Better methods of desalination have to be developed to make it viable for meeting freshwater needs in the future.

In addition, the rapid growth of Dubai has caused problems with its waste disposal system. The nearby beaches and sea have become highly polluted by human sewage in recent years. This poses a threat not only to human health but also to marine life.

by the hustle and bustle of city life, or the chance to get rich. In some cases, governments have forced nomadic people to settle because their independent, border-crossing lifestyle means that they are not loyal to one particular country. And in other cases, big oil and gas companies have bought up and developed ancestral lands, forcing the inhabitants to go elsewhere.

But adjusting to city life can also be hard, especially for people in poor countries. Many of the Saharan Tuareg people, for example, now live in shantytowns on the outskirts of towns such as Tombouctou, in Mali. Some survive by selling souvenirs and camel rides to tourists, and many others work in offices or factories. Some Tuareg people miss their old, freer way of life, which they call *adima*, meaning "far from the town."

Mongolian herders—like all desert peoples—remain experts at making the best of whatever their environment has to offer. In the Gobi desert, the Mongolian herders continue to migrate from pastureland to pastureland and live in their distinctive tents, called *gers* or yurts. One big difference, though, is that many herders now round up their flocks on motorbikes instead of on horseback.

The lack of snow in the desert does not discourage snow boarders. The ride is bumpy and short, but a lot of fun. Other adventurous desert sports include sand sledding and dune bashing in dune buggies.

Although it brings in wealth to many poor regions, tourism in deserts impacts on wildlife. Off-road vehicles can cause much damage, especially to slow-growing plants and lichens (life-forms consisting of a fungus and an alga) in semiarid regions.

GOBI AND TAKLA MAKAN

The cold deserts of China and Mongolia experience extreme temperatures and bitter winters as well as scant rainfall. Despite this, herdspeople and traveling traders have crossed these deserts for thousands of years.

Beasts of Burden

In the Gobi and Takla Makan lives the two-humped Bactrian camel. It has the long eyelashes, large, splaying feet, and closable nostrils of other camels, but it also has a long, shaggy coat to protect it from the winter cold. Most Bactrian camels are kept by people, but there are still a few wild herds left in the remote areas of Mongolia and China. A camel's ability to lose a quarter of its body weight in water has been useful to people wanting to cross deserts. For centuries traders and their camels crossed the Gobi and Takla Makan in groups called caravans. They carried silk and spices from China to Europe. Today, camels are still useful to desert people. The camel on the right is waiting outside its owner's dwelling, a canvas and felt tent called a yurt, or *ger*.

Karakorum

2   5   Altai Shan (mountains)

M O N G O L I A

N

▲ Bogda Feng
nqi

Turpan Depression
Turpan   4

Yelyn Valley → 6

Erenhot

G   o   b   i

3   Gansu Desert

Lop
i River Nur

C H I N A

Ala Shan desert

Huang He (Yellow River)

!

7   Baotou   Hohhot

Datong

tun Shan (mountains) ▲ Altun Shan

Tengger desert

Wuhai

Mu Us desert

Yinchuan

Muztag Feng

P l a t e a u

0 ——— 200 miles
0 ——— 200 km

The Gobi is dominated by vast, treeless wastes. Its gray-brown surface is sparsely covered with hardy grass and bushes. Here, sand dunes dwarf a pair of yurts.

1. Tarim Basin
This region lies in the rain shadow of towering mountains on three sides, and very little rain reaches it. Around the rim, some rivers flow. They are fed by groundwater welling up and by snow melting on the mountains. Global warming is increasing the rate at which the snow melts and the flow of the rivers.

2. Dzungarian Basin
Where Przewalski's horses, the last truly wild horses, roamed until the 1960s. Overgrazing by livestock and overconsumption and pollution of water threaten the wildlife in this region.

3. Lop Nur Salt Marsh
The Konqi River evaporates away in the desert Sun, creating this salty marshland. Rare wild

Bactrian camels are under threat from hunters in this region.

4. Turpan Depression
The lowest-lying and hottest place in China, with a record temperature of 47°C (117°F).

5. Altai Shan
A mountain refuge of the endangered snow leopard. Overgrazing by livestock threatens the ibex, the snow leopard's main prey.

6. Yelyn Valley
A national park whose craggy cliffs are home to vultures.

7. Huang He (Yellow River)
This great river skirts the edge of the Gobi and irrigates a large area of farmland. Pollution in the river affects wildlife.

Gobi Facts

▲ There are hardly any roads in the Gobi, but the bare rock and gravel terrain is often so flat and even that you can drive a car for long distances in any direction.

▲ Some large mammals scrape a living in the Gobi, including the two-humped Bactrian camel, the Asiatic wild ass, and the Mongolian gazelle. Illegal hunting threatens these animals.

▲ The Takla Makan desert is mainly covered in windblown sand. In the eastern foothills of the Tian Shan mountains, the sand dunes reach heights of 200–300 meters (650–1,000 feet).

THE FUTURE FOR DESERTS

Earth's climate has been changing throughout history, and it will continue to change. Deserts naturally expand and shrink, and even disappear.

Satellites are helping monitor desertification around the world. This image from the European Space Agency (ESA) shows land degradation in Sudan, Africa.

Algeria is now a desert country, but it was not always so. In the center of Algeria, near a place called Aouinet, there are caves where people lived about 5,500 years ago. The cave dwellers decorated their walls with paintings of everyday activities. These showed them herding cattle and hunting hippopotamuses from canoes. Some pictures are even earlier. They show elephants, buffalo, and rhinoceroses. Clearly, the Sahara was not a desert then.

Thousands of years from now, the Sahara might be forest again, and all deserts might be different. But what about the near future?

Global Warming

Most scientists now agree that the world's climates are growing warmer because of the enhanced greenhouse effect of increased carbon dioxide and other greenhouse gases in the atmosphere. In a warmer world, rainfall might increase in what are now dry countries. If scientists are right, some present-day deserts might disappear and new ones might form. The Sahara, the Thar Desert in India, and the deserts of southwest Asia could vanish altogether. The Australian deserts would not disappear, though, because they are caused partly by their distance from the ocean. But they might get smaller. Before long, livestock would be able to graze in what are now barren wastelands. And once a layer of soil had formed, farmers could grow crops.

New and Old Deserts

In other places, life might become more difficult for people. Parts of the central United States and southern Europe could become drier—they could turn into new deserts. However, warming can also lead in

Climate Change

Some gases in the atmosphere, such as carbon dioxide and methane, act a bit like the glass windows of a greenhouse. They let the Sun's warmth pass in, but they trap the heat rays coming from the sunshine-warmed ground. This phenomenon is known as the greenhouse effect. Cars, airplanes, and factories belch out extra quantities of these greenhouse gases. The increased greenhouse gases are changing Earth's climate. Although some countries are getting warmer, others are getting wetter, stormier, or even colder. For instance, global warming is disrupting the ocean currents that keep Europe's climate mild, and Great Britain might one day become as cold as northern Canada.

The vast majority of scientists now agree that unless countries work together to bring down their emissions of greenhouse gases, global warming and climate change will continue with drastic effects for humans and wildlife.

If global warming continues, deserts in the United States could expand. Semiarid prairie could become as dry as the scene below.

some places to more evaporation, more clouds, and wetter conditions. In these places, farming conditions would improve.

The west-coast deserts, such as the Namib and Atacama, will probably remain much as they are now—unless there is a big change in the circulation of the oceans. Some scientists fear that warmer air and increased rainfall might alter the ocean currents. If that were

Desertification

Some dry lands are not deserts, since they receive enough rainfall to support dry scrub or grassland. Herdspeople graze their animals on the grassland, but the grazing is in short supply. Particularly in dry years, overgrazing happens: animals strip the leaves from shrubs and eat grass right down to the ground. The baked, dry soil, stripped of its protective plant covering, blows away in clouds of dust. The soil can no longer support the scrubby plants, and the land becomes a desert. This process, termed desertification, is caused not only by overgrazing. It can also happen when people divert rivers elsewhere as part of an irrigation project, for instance. Desertified land cannot recover unless people return its water supply and reduce the number of grazing animals.

In some desert locations, such as Jabal Tuwayq (above) in Saudi Arabia, people draw water from deep underground to irrigate crops. The crops grow in circles because they are watered by a pivoting sprinkler. The circular fields can be more than 1.6 kilometers (1 mile) across.

to happen, the cold currents flowing along the west coasts of the continents might weaken, allowing a layer of warm water to form above them. The Atacama and Sonoran deserts might then become wet and stormy.

If a desert changes into fertile pasture or cropland, or if farmland turns into desert, then the lives of the people living there will alter dramatically. They will have to learn new skills. Traveling nomads might have to become farmers, while farmers elsewhere might be forced to abandon their dusty fields and find other places to live.

Farming the Desert

If the climate does change, there are ways to prevent farmland from turning into desert. Trees planted in lines can shield land from the wind so that the ground dries more slowly and is less likely to get buried by dust and sand. Crops can be grown between lines of trees, and leaves from the trees can be fed to livestock. This is called corridor farming. Rain in the desert is often so heavy that it washes soil off hillsides, but people can stop this from happening by building low walls from the stones that are common in rocky deserts. The stone walls stop mud from running straight downhill and allow soil to build up behind the walls.

In dry parts of the United States, people have figured out a system of dry farming. After a crop has been harvested, the field is left bare but plowed occasionally to kill and bury any weeds. After three years, the rotting weeds have nourished the soil enough for a new crop to be sown. It is even possible to grow trees on the slopes of a sand dune. First a coating of oil and rubber is sprayed on the dune to bind sand grains together. Then tree seedlings are planted through holes in the coating. Certain types of eucalyptus and acacia trees are particularly suitable—they can grow where less than 150 millimeters (6 inches) of rain falls every year.

The soil in many desert areas is too salty for most crop plants, but certain plants, such as date palms and some varieties of almond tree, can tolerate a lot of salt. Some hardy plants, such as glasswort and sea blite, can even be watered with

Sahara Resources

People use the dry lands around the fringes of the Sahara for grazing sheep, goats, and cattle. Beyond the desert, on the Mediterranean coast, the climate is wet enough to grow citrus fruits and olives. Farmers use the well-watered, fertile Nile Valley for growing a range of crops. The heart of the desert is mainly empty, but there are occasional oases where people harvest dates.

Oases with date palms

Olive groves

Cotton fields

Citrus fruit orchards

Sugar beet fields

Pastureland

seawater. Farm animals will eat some of these plants, and others can be processed to make industrial materials, such as oils.

Desert Peoples

Until recently, many of the world's deserts and semideserts were home to nomads. But the nomadic way of life is now disappearing quickly. A dramatic change has already happened in the Persian Gulf, where large, modern cities sprang up in the desert after oil

was discovered. Many of the residents now enjoy a lifestyle that their grandparents couldn't have imagined.

Similar changes are happening throughout the world's deserts, though less quickly. The Sahel is a wide band of dry grassland and scrub along the southern edge of the Sahara. Governments of countries in the Sahel have encouraged the nomadic people there to settle. The governments drilled bore holes to bring water from deep underground, and provided better medical and veterinary care. People now keep many more animals and graze them continuously around their villages. This new lifestyle is risky because when droughts happen, the herdspeople cannot move on to graze their animals elsewhere. The animals overgraze the land, and famine may follow.

Most deserts are remote from large cities and major roads. With cell phones, radio, TV, and now the Internet, however, desert people know what is happening beyond the desert and can keep in touch. It is now much easier for these people to be integrated into the global community.

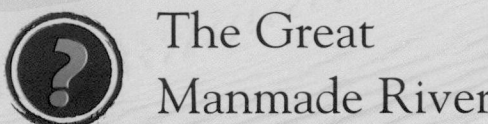

The Great Manmade River

The country of Libya in northern Africa is made up almost entirely of desert, and most Libyans live in a thin, fertile strip of land along the coast of the Mediterranean Sea. Even on the coast, however, there is barely enough rain for crops to grow and cattle to graze cattle, and drought is common.

Far beneath the blazing-hot surface of the Libyan Desert is a vast reservoir of water, trapped in a layer of absorbent rock. Much of this water trickled down thousands of years ago, before the Sahara became a desert. In the 1980s, the Libyan government began a huge project—the Great Manmade River Project—to tap the water and pump it to coastal cities. More than 200 gigantic wells are being built in the Sahara, with a combined depth of 620 kilometers (385 miles)—70 times the height of Mount Everest. Some of the wells are already in operation. These reserves of desert water should last several hundreds years.

The Future

No one knows what the world will be like a century from now. The predictions of climate change are based on calculations made by climatologists (scientists who study climates). Because of global warming, most predictions for deserts are not good. At the worst, desert temperatures will rise by up to 7°C (12.6°F) and rainfall will drop by up to 20 percent (unless nations across the world act together to halt climate change and global warming). Most deserts seem likely to change, and perhaps new ones will appear. The change in temperature will affect the plants and animals that have evolved in the desert. Some may thrive; others will struggle to survive.

Deserts are great places for generating energy from the wind and Sun. This array of solar collectors converts sunlight into electricity. However, there is a downside: areas of fragile desert vegetation are cleared to build these power stations.

GLOSSARY

acacia: A type of tree or shrub, common in semideserts of Africa and Australia, that often has small leaflets and thorns.

amphibian: A cold-blooded animal that spends part of its life in water and part on land, such as a frog or salamander.

aquifer: A large supply of water trapped deep underground.

arid: Having a very dry climate. Deserts are arid.

atmosphere: The layer of air around Earth.

Bedouin: Nomadic Arabs who live in the deserts of southwest Asia and North Africa.

biome: A major division of the living world, distinguished by its climate and wildlife. Tundra and deserts are examples of biomes.

camouflage: Natural disguise that makes animals or plants look like their surroundings.

caravan: A line of vehicles or pack animals traveling together through difficult terrain.

carbon dioxide: A gas released when fuel burns. Carbon dioxide is one of the main gases causing global warming.

climate: The pattern of weather that happens in one place during an average year.

cold-blooded: Having a body temperature that depends on the surroundings. Reptiles are cold-blooded, for example. *See also* warm-blooded.

desert: A place that receives less than 250 millimeters (10 inches) of rain a year.

desertification: The process of becoming desertlike. It can happen naturally or because of human interference.

domestic animal: An animal kept by people, usually as a pet, farm animal, or pack animal.

dormant: So inactive as to appear lifeless. Plant seeds often stay dormant until their soil gets wet.

ephemeral: A plant with a very short life cycle that appears only occasionally, such as a desert poppy.

equator: An imaginary line around Earth, midway between the poles.

evaporate: To turn from liquid into gas. When water evaporates, it becomes an invisible part of the air.

excretion: The removal by animals or plants of chemical wastes from inside their cells.

fertile: Capable of sustaining plant growth. Farmers often try to make soil more fertile when growing crops.

global warming: The gradual warming of Earth's climate, thought to be caused by pollution of the atmosphere.

ice age: A period in history when Earth's climate was cooler and the polar ice caps expanded. The last ice age ended about 10,000 years ago.

irrigation: The use of channeled water by people to grow plants in dry areas.

migration: A long-distance journey by an animal to find a new home. Many animals migrate each year.

nitrate: A mineral that helps plants grow.

nomad: A person who travels from place to place in search of food and water, instead of settling permanently.

oasis: An area where there is enough water to sustain plants, but is surrounded by desert.

polar desert: The main biome in Antarctica, northernmost Canada, and Greenland. Polar desert gets very little rain or snow, and the ground is usually barren or covered with ice.

pollination: The transfer of pollen from the male part of a flower to the female part of the same flower or another flower, causing the flower to produce seeds.

prairie: A large area of grassland in central North America.

predator: An animal that catches and eats other animals.

rain forest: A lush forest that receives frequent heavy rainfall. Tropical rain forests grow in the tropics; temperate rain forests grow in cooler places.

rain shadow: An area where rainfall is low because nearby mountains provide shelter from rain-bearing winds.

salt flat: A flat area covered with salt left behind by evaporation.

salt pan: A natural depression in which water collects and evaporates, leaving behind salt.

semiarid: Having a dry climate, but not as dry as a desert. Semiarid areas receive 250–510 millimeters (10–20 inches) of rain each year.

semidesert: A dry area that is not as dry as a desert. Semidesert is most common around the fringes of deserts.

shrubland: A biome that mainly contains shrubs, such as the chaparral of California.

species: A particular type of organism. Cheetahs are a species, for instance, but birds are not, because there are lots of different bird species.

succulent: A plant with juicy, fleshy tissue. Cacti are succulents.

taiga: A biome in northern regions that mainly contains conifer trees.

temperate: Between the warm tropics and the cold, polar regions.

temperate forest: A biome of the temperate zone that mainly contains broadleaf trees.

temperate grassland: A biome of the temperate zone that mainly contains grassland. The U.S. prairie is part of the temperate grassland biome.

tropic of Cancer: An imaginary line around Earth about 2,600 kilometers (1,600 miles) north of the equator. From here, the Sun appears directly overhead at noon on June 21.

tropic of Capricorn: An imaginary line around Earth about 2,600 kilometers (1,600 miles) south of the equator. From here, the Sun is directly overhead at noon on December 21.

tropical: Between the tropics of Cancer and Capricorn. Tropical countries are warm all year.

tropical forest: Forest growing in Earth's tropical zone, such as tropical rain forest or monsoon forest.

tropical grassland: A tropical biome that mainly contains grassland, such as savanna.

tundra: A biome of the far north, made up of treeless plains covered with small plants.

warm-blooded: Having a constantly warm body temperature. Mammals and birds are warm-blooded.

water vapor: The gas that forms when water evaporates.

Further Research

Books

Greenberger, R. *Deserts (Biomes of the World)*. New York: Rosen Central, 2009.
Gritzner, Charles, F. *Deserts (Extreme Environments)*. New York: Chelsea House, 2006.
MacQuitty, Miranda. *Eyewitness Desert*. New York: DK Inc., 2000.
Martin, Michael. *Deserts of the Earth*. New York: Thames & Hudson, 2004.

Websites

United States National Park Service: www.nps.gov/parks.html
(Includes information on Saguaro National Park and Mojave National Preserve.)
Living Eden: www.pbs.org/edens
(Covers the Namib, Canyonlands, and Etosha.)
Cool Planet: www.oxfam.org.uk/coolplanet/ontheline/explore/nature/deserts/deserts.htm
(Offers an introduction to the geography, wildlife, and climate of deserts.)
Desert Topics: www.mbgnet.net/sets/desert/index.htm.
(Fun website answering questions about deserts.)

INDEX

Page numbers in *italics* refer to picture captions.

Picture Credits

Key: l – left, r – right, m – middle, t – top, b – bottom.

Front cover: istockphoto. **Ardea:** 24b; John Canaclosi 8b; Thomas Dressler 41; Francois Gohier 1, 15, 16b, 25, 36b, 54; Ken Lucas 34t; Stefan Meyers 32; Peter Steyn 27; M. Watson 7m, 11; C. Weaver 48; Alan Weaving 24t; Wardene Weisser 23t; Art Explosion: 13t, 29t; **Bruce Coleman:** Jules Cowan 16t; Jeff Foott 6m, 29; Carol Hughes 37; Joe McDonald 40b; Rod Williams 39b; **Corbis:** Yann Arthus-Bertrand 30, 56 (inset), 59; Dean Conger 7r, 55; Richard Cummins 47b; Michael and Patricia Fogden 36t; Gallo Images 13m; **Image Bank:** Jean AEF Duboisberranger 45b, 53b; Frans Lemmens 7r, 43, 51; Ben Weaver 53m; **European Space Agency:** 56t; **istockphoto:** 23b, 28b, 34b; NASA: 10, 45t, 58t; **NHPA:** A.N.T. 40t; A.N.T./Grant Dixon 6r, 19; Anthony Bannister 28, 46; Nigel J. Dennis 21b, 58b; Douglas Dickins 50; Patrick Fagot 21; Daniel Heuclin 42; John Shaw 47t; **PhotoDisc:** Neil Beer 35; Robert Glusic 4m, 22, 56–57; Bruce Heinemann 5l; Jack Hollingsworth 5m; Photolink 5r, 8t; Karl Weatherly 4r; **Shutterstock:** Bryan Busovicki 17m; Barnaby Chambers 41 (inset); Ostill 43m; Yanir Taflev 61; **South American Pictures:** Chris Sharp 18.

The Brown Reference Group Ltd has made every attempt to contact the copyright holder. If anyone has any information please contact info@brownreference.com